Win It, Drive It!

The Tools You Need to Win Interviews and Drive Your Career

MK DUPUIS

Copyright © 2020 MK DUPUIS

All rights reserved.

ISBN: 9798559347004

First Edition

No part of this book may be used or reproduced in any manner whatsoever without the publisher's prior written permission, except in the case of brief quotations embodied in reviews.

DEDICATION

I'm dedicating this book to all the outstanding leaders I knew or reported to over the years. To some of the top leaders at the Nielsen Company from the past as well. That group starts with Arthur Nielsen Sr. and Arthur Nielsen Jr. Those two leaders demonstrated the ability to have significant power and authority yet wield it like a loving and wise parent. It made you feel like part of the family, which generated dedication and loyalty. They were also all about innovation, personal development and making sure that "everybody wins." Find leaders like them to follow, then become one of them!

CONTENT

Chapter 1: Introduction   1

Chapter 2: Understanding the Contents' Impact on You   22
    9-Box Matrix   23

Chapter 3: How to Improve Your Chances for Success   34
    Differentiation   34
    Skill Set Matrix   36
    SMART Goals   46
    ATS, HR and the Interview   57

Chapter 4: Level 1 Thinking   68
    Think in a New Box   69
    Right-to-Left Thinking   70
    Lean Six Sigma   75
    Thought Leadership   90
    Diversity and Unconscious Bias   92
    Cultural Differences Human Similarities   97

Chapter 5: Level 2 Thinking   102
    Project Planning   102
    Time Management   111
    Dangers of Multitasking   114
    Persuasion and Negotiation   123

Chapter 6: Connecting with Others   128
    Effective Listening   131
    Networking   134
    Team Player and Teamwork   140
    Mentoring   144
    Being Remotely Managed   146

Chapter 7: Performance Reviews   155
    What and How   156
    Difficult Feedback   159

Chapter 8: Leadership   **162**
    Operating Like a Leader   175
    Perseverance   180
    Motivation   182

Chapter 9: Tool Synopsis   **188**

Chapter 10: How to Make It All Work   **195**

Chapter 11: Where to Go from Here?   **201**

CHAPTER 1

INTRODUCTION

To me, everyone who buys this book is a client of mine. Due to that, my purpose is to bring you a great return on your investment. A return not only for your financial investment but for your investment of time. As well, I hope to entertain you with some of the stories from my career. I'll remind you again at the end of this book, but I'd like to hear from you either in reviews or emails (winitdriveit@gmail.com) on how this information helped you. I do anticipate hearing from you more than once. Why? Because you will be able to use this advice for years and across multiple situations. Your feedback helps confirm that your time and effort in reading the book has been valuable to you. In sending out a survey afterwards, I'd want 100% of the responses to be "Very Satisfied."

I wrote this first edition during the global pandemic. The virus has created a recession and impacted the global economy, affecting people differently based on their station in life. As stated by an investment strategist, "Many millennials — if not most — entered the job market during one of these recent recessions, struggling to find work and build a career in an incredibly competitive labour market." A key recommendation he made for millennials, and Gen Z was to "Invest in your human capital through education and skills development." Very sound advice and, that's the kind of action you will take by reading this book and working through the exercises. The labour market is extremely competitive, becoming more so each day through technology and globalization. You need the edge that I'm looking to provide you.

In purchasing this book, you have taken a step that is critically important to remember. Namely, "It is your responsibility to drive your career!" You might feel that this statement is obvious. However, I've met many people who didn't think in this way much, if at all. Here's a question for you. What have you done in the last six months to drive your career? Have you thought about that question lately, or ever? You need to recognize this, remember it, and <u>actively</u> manage it. In a way, you are the sole proprietor responsible for running a business, which is "you." Like a business owner, you need to map out plans for the year and determine where people (you) need training. You also need to undertake regular reviews to see how the business is tracking against the plan. You're responsible for the marketing plan to attract attention to your business. It's also your responsibility to ensure that the business grows year over year. Bottom line, even if you work for someone else your entire career, you can still think of yourself as a sole proprietor and make sure to do the greatest possible job to make your business (you) successful.

Win It, Drive It!

There are many people out there, maybe even you at this point, thinking that new job opportunities or promotions will just automatically pop up for them. They believe that just showing up for work every day and doing a good job will make things happen for them. Yes, you do need to show up every day and do a good job, but there's a lot more to it than that. Yes, head-hunters do proactively go after some employees. However, the number of people getting new opportunities that way is minuscule. Besides that, ironically, they're getting noticed due to how they are driving their career. So, if your mindset has been "show up and work hard" and nothing has happened for you, the great news is that you're now going to start driving your career based on a new mindset from this book.

The superior value of all the different types of advice here is that it's not locked to a specific job, department, company, nor industry. The guidance applies everywhere! This information is what we call transferrable knowledge and skills, meaning you can take it and leverage it no matter where you go in your career. I consistently recommended to the people reporting to me to always take advantage of training opportunities that involved transferrable knowledge and skills. Even though the training was to help them on the job today, it would still assist them if they moved to a new role, department, or company. An extra benefit is that you can utilize most of the information in your personal life. That will deliver additional value for your time and effort to read and absorb this material. It should repay you a thousand times over. A final word on usefulness to you is that this advice is timeless. No matter how many years from now someone picks up this book, things like leadership, planning, self-reflection, or skill development will still be just as valuable and relevant then.

Why do I know that this advice can help millions of people? Here are four key reasons:

1. I've had many conversations with my direct reports over the years sharing these kinds of details, and I've seen it help them to be successful. Many other people, like my direct reports, are not aware of this information.

    I also agreed to act as a career advisor on LinkedIn (LI) and was notified other members sought guidance. In the last few months, I saw six people asking for advice in finding jobs without putting any real effort into thinking through where they truly wanted to go. I'll talk about this more later on, but they are all in desperate need of this advice!

2. I'm sharing much of the knowledge gained through my leadership roles over the years. In those positions, I've made decisions on who to hire, promote or fire! I made hiring decisions through a series of questions. For the promotion or fire decisions, I arrived at them through observations of performance <u>and character</u>.

    When you work in a leadership role, it provides you with a very different perspective and forces you to develop yourself more. It's like the difference between being single and being married with children. While you may think and do many things the same way, the married person with children must develop and look at things differently because of their new and expanded responsibilities. A key one is a consideration for others rather than just focusing on themselves and their needs.

3. After my corporate career ended, I took a position as a part-time college professor. My first class consisted of post-graduate students, with the course being on Leadership and Management Fundamentals. I found the textbook and pre-set presentation material saturated in terms of content. It seemed like the book had a lot of filler information to justify its excessively high price. There were two times during the course where slides talked about a specific leadership style; then the last one said, "But many people don't feel this style is relevant anymore." Guess which slides I removed from the deck rather than show the students.

   While the content was instructive, I felt it was more suited to people about to embark on a leadership role. These were students who would be several years away from such a position. I started by sharing with the students that it was most valuable for them to understand how leadership should operate. However, I added the caveat that some people in leadership roles do not perform as great leaders. Sometimes it's the exact opposite, but I won't name names! By understanding how leadership looks at people, what they need to accomplish and their challenges, you could gain visibility and favour with their leadership. Not in a "kiss up" kind of way, but in a functionally proper and supportive way. On the other side of the coin, I cautioned that if they found that leadership was not functioning this way, it was a red flag and should prompt them to move on. It's highly stressful, demoralizing, and unpleasant to work for a toxic boss.

4. Finally, I self-reflected, looked to change for the better (Kaizen) and stayed curious. I tested my ability to stretch myself and write this book. I knew that many things I learned later in my career would have been valuable to know in the

early days. This book will give you a head start that I never had.

Decisively, it was teaching those young people in college that turned on the light for this books' value. Often in class, I would share a story from my career. At times I would say, "This will be helpful to you from day one on the job, so make sure to write this down." Those are the kinds of things I will share here.

This simple instruction in class made it easy to pick out which students would be successful down the road and who would not achieve <u>their potential</u>. Without them realizing it, that moment was a live example of something a leader does to see whom they will select for extraordinary opportunities. It also decides whom they will never spend much of their valuable time on. If you're new or struggling with a challenge, a good leader will put in time with you. However, if you show that you don't care much about the job, why should a leader care about giving their time to you? They need to spend their time and share their expertise with people <u>who will make a difference</u>.

Those who didn't write anything down were typically not taking any notes but socializing and checking their phones. As time passed, it was apparent that they were only aiming to coast through school and life. Sadly, it will be these same people who, down the road, will not be successful and spend their time blaming life and others for their misery. They will become jealous of their colleagues who succeed and get promoted. They will think that life isn't fair. Life isn't fair at times, but don't say it isn't if you're lazy and ignoring advice. You had the same opportunity as everyone else in the room!

In teaching these students, I shared many of the insights that I often shared with people reporting to me. Many of the topics here I also shared with individuals or my team. When any leader in any business spends the time teaching this content, it creates benefits connecting four groups as follows:

1. If the employees learn this new knowledge or skill, they can be more productive and efficient, increasing their job satisfaction.
2. If the teams' skills expand, their performance improves, reducing headaches for the leader and makes the leader look better to those above.
3. With teams performing better and improved job satisfaction, the company can be more successful, cut or hold costs to improve profitability and have lower turnover, saving money. These improvements should benefit clients through better quality, faster and consistent delivery, and keeping prices reasonable.
4. For shareholders, a well-performing business should provide a more significant return on their investment and keep their investment stable.

So, training and sharing knowledge help the individuals, the business, their clients, and the shareholders. Everybody wins, and that's what we should all want.

Is this book just for individuals? In one sense, the obvious answer is "Yes." However, it is also quite valuable for a small business owner to utilize this knowledge across all their employees. Why? Small businesses typically do not have an HR department. Nor do they usually have staff training programs outside of the "This is how to do your specific job" type of training. Yet, a real difference can be made for that small business if every one of their employees would know and deliver against the knowledge contained here. After all, I was learning and teaching my staff these things while working in a global corporation. The purpose was to help the team and myself become more innovative, better problem solvers, and more efficient. In doing so, we could create new ideas and help cut costs to improve profitability. Now, what small business doesn't want to or need to, do the same? And those are the things I know this book can help deliver.

To get a high-level feel for the content, assume that you, and five other candidates, are being interviewed. All six of you have the same experience, hard skills, and soft skills. You're all dressed the same and come across in the same pleasing way. The only difference between all of you is that in the interview, only you can share knowledge of items such as Six Sigma, right-to-left thinking, 9-Box Matrix application, and project planning, growth mindset. You can share how this knowledge will help you make a difference. Whom do you think the company would hire? Yes, congratulations, it's you!

This time you're in charge of an important project at work, having to pick between two equal people. One of them knows about Six Sigma, right-to-left thinking, and project planning, while the other had no clue about these things. Whom would you pick?

Later, I will discuss differentiation, and these last two questions have highlighted what that means. It's about two people being the same across many metrics, but there are areas where one person differentiates themselves. And that helps to make the final, impactful decision!

Before going any further, I need to highlight a few things that will be very important for you to commit to. As well, if you're not willing to commit, you should put the book down. Firstly, I mentioned it earlier, and you will see this included later; "It's your job to drive your career." Next, you must be committed to continuing to work on applying the advice until you achieve your first success. Once you do that, use it as momentum and motivation to keep on performing. At the back of the book, I provided a "Success Log" to track how the different advice pieces have helped. I hope you have so many successes over the years that you'll quickly fill the log and need to use an external document to keep it going! I also hope you will dedicate a lifetime commitment to the advice. Finally, I would ask that each year, on the anniversary of you starting to read this book, that you review your Success Log and self-reflect on how much you've grown in that year. Then after that self-reflection, go out and celebrate! You've earned it. So, before you forget, put a recurring, annual reminder in your calendar for one year from now.

When you look at the building blocks of skills, the foundation consists of different intelligence types like analytic and creative, personality traits, plus your values and interests. While you can change these things over time, it isn't easy to do so. The blocks of knowledge and experience are above that foundation, and then the top row is competencies and skills. These blocks are much easier to change, and it's the advice in this book that will help guide you to improvements. Some guidance is for a skill, some are knowledge, and some for a state of mind. For simplicity's sake, let's think of all these pieces of advice as tools. You're the contractor, and the long-term job is building your career. You have a large toolbox, and over time, you're going to add several tools to help in the building process. You won't be using all the tools all the time, only when needed. However, like any good and successful worker, you must take care of your tools to optimize your performance. Sometimes your current model is out of date, so you need to get the new and improved model. Again, you're the contractor, your career is the job, and these are the tools you need.

I'm going to share with you a high-level description of the No Limit Holdem poker game. Hopefully, then, the word, "poker," will remind you in the future of some of my advice. What is the connection that game and this book? A famous saying amongst the best players in the world is, "Poker is not a game of cards played by people; it's a game of people played with cards." What do you think that means?

Here's a description of the "mechanics" of the game. Every deal uses the same deck of 52 cards every single time, forever. There are precisely 1,326 combinations of cards that you could receive in the deal. Like the number of cards in the deck, this number never changes. After each player gets their two cards, there is a betting round. After this, the dealer puts three cards face up. There is another betting round, and the dealer turns up a fourth card, another betting round, and the dealer turns up a fifth and final card. After the final card comes up, there is one more round of betting. And if more than one player is still involved after the last betting round, it will be the cards that determine the winner.

The description to this point is only looking at the card aspect of the game. So, where does the people part come into play? The professionals are continually paying attention to the other people at the table. They are watching for their betting patterns, how they react to other players' bets and any physical "tells" that provide them with information. They use this knowledge to begin categorizing their opponents. They determine who is a weak player and play aggressively against them. The weak player may check or make a minimum bet and, regardless of the strength of their hand, the professional makes a large enough bet that the weak player folds perhaps a winning hand. This move is the best example of it being a "game of people played with cards" rather than "a game of cards played by people." In this case, the cards had nothing to do with the outcome; it was the professionals' assessment of their opponent.

Another thought process that poker players are consciously doing during a game relates to self-reflection. As much as the players categorize their opponents, they also think deeply about how their opponents view them. They also know that their opponents are looking at them in different ways. The weak players may not be categorizing them correctly, if at all. The better players will have a good read, in any case. They will then make specific bets and moves in the game based on how they think the opponent in that hand is viewing them.

Do you have a good feel for how people at work are categorizing you? Do they think of you as being innovative and valuable? Do they think of you as a team player or someone they wouldn't want on their team? This process is much like first impressions being used to bucket people. Everyone does it. We meet someone new and start categorizing them quickly. So, like the poker players, you need to be continually and consciously assessing how other people are thinking about you. Have you carried yourself in a way that ensures they have the right image? More importantly, are you projecting this image continually? Everyone can occasionally project a positive impression, but only those who are the real deal can do so consistently.

There are many other nuances to the game that make it fascinating. Even with a great read on people, you still need to utilize data. Players consider numerous facts such as the pot size, their stack (chips), plus the blinds and antes. If they think they're currently behind in the hand, they then calculate the chance of getting a card to improve their hand value to a winning position. That is, if they know a bet on its' own, no matter how large, will not get their opponent to fold.

However, the key is assessing people, including yourself, making decisions and acting based on that assessment. They are acting like leaders because they're taking into consideration facts and people. The relevance to you is that leadership is doing this at work all the time as well. They will regularly look at metrics to see that angle of your performance. They are continually assessing people during interactions and categorizing everyone into buckets from weak to outstanding. When opportunities or promotions come along, they have a very narrow group of people to consider, and you want to be in that group! A suggestion, then, is to have the word "poker" in a visible place to remind yourself that people are assessing you each day. So, you always want to be at the top of your game.

Getting the maximum benefit from this book will require more than just memorizing the content and recalling it as needed. Sure, you will need to remember different elements from time to time, but the maximum benefit will be to operate with the necessary mindset actively and repeatedly. The more often you can work in this mindset and make it an active way of going about things, the better. Making this adjustment will be difficult if you're overloaded and continuously distracted by life. However, items of value are never easy, and you can do it!

One of the central themes in this book is differentiation. If you can shift yourself into operating with this new mindset, it will differentiate you from the masses. From the people who are so stuck in their way of doing things, "they can't see the forest for the trees." If you haven't heard that saying before, it means that you can no longer see the big picture (forest) as you are focused on so many small details (trees).

To get into, and maintain, the right mindset, which will be the engine to drive everything else, let's use these few words as our guiding light; "Kaizen + Self-reflection + Stay Curious." Let's call it "Kaisersc" (Kaiser-sk) for simplicity. An understanding of each is as follows:

Kaizen – A Japanese term meaning "change for the better." Due to its' uses in the business world, you may also hear it referred to as a term for "continuous improvement." In addition to the fact that I include it in this mindset, you will also see it referenced later when we look at Six Sigma as a tool. You should look to lead a "life of Kaizen" for the rest of your life. Look to change for the better consistently.

Self-reflection – You will need to do this whenever you have an annual performance review, are preparing for an interview, are thinking of changing jobs, or are wanting to follow "Kaizen." It's something that all leaders do to get where they are, so it's something you need to do as well. However, to ensure you aren't missing self-change opportunities due to your blind spots, self-reflection needs to be supported by 360 feedback that we'll discuss later.

Stay Curious – Only two words, but very valuable. Curious is defined in the dictionary as "eager to know or learn something." Curiosity will help you get into experiences or great joys as it will take you outside your comfort zone. And, as they often say, "that's where life begins!" In short order, I'll give a high-level view of my career, which shows how curiosity enabled it to be one that was very interesting and personally fulfilling.

KAISERSC

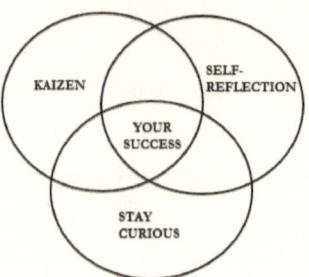

I've settled upon this mindset combination based on what happened across my career. To be clear, I never made it to the level of CEO or President or Vice-President. I was never a "highflyer" in the corporate world, but that's okay in this case. Why? There are many books out there about becoming a corporate leader, a millionaire, or a world-class entrepreneur. While you may become one of those people someday (I hope), around 95% of the population will not. However, the 95% group still has a great desire to become successful and happy. Those are the people I'm looking to help. I want to make a difference for them in a positive way no matter the incremental size gain as long as it's positive.

What did my career look like, and how did it demonstrate Kaizen, Self-Reflection and Stay Curious? Read on and look to see different ways of thinking or approaches to situations you may face today or in the future. Would you have been able to work through these things in the same way that I did? Perhaps yes, perhaps no. If no, trust that you can shift your mindset. You will be able to think and react in different, more powerful, and successful ways that as time passes.

I started with the AC Nielsen Company back in the mid-70s as a Field Representative. During my time in that department, I gained more responsibility and leadership experience in an external role. After a promotion into the office, I moved into a variety of roles. The one I enjoyed the most was conducting a test of hand-held terminals. The task was to determine if they could replace the paper and pencil routine for gathering inventory information from retail stores. This project was the first time where my curiosity was invaluable.

The department lead tasked me to conduct a productivity test between the two methods. Pretty early on, it became evident that the terminal was significantly faster than paper and pencil. I realized that the responsibility for product identification moving from my hands to an internal coding team was the main reason. Yes, I was responsible for ensuring that the price, quantity, and any display credit was accurate for the UPC bar code (Universal Product Code, known as EAN elsewhere) that I scanned. However, I had no idea if the system had that UPC coded to the correct item. Curiosity led me to undertake some quality checks on top of the productivity tests.

By the agreed deadline, I wrote a full report on the test outcome. I also prepared and presented my findings to a leadership team, including the President of AC Nielsen Canada. Stating that there was a significant 35% productivity increase brought great smiles to the room. However, my next statement was that I did not recommend implementing the equipment just yet due to serious quality concerns. Naturally, I quickly followed that statement with examples of what I had found in my "curiosity" checks.

Everyone in the room agreed with my conclusions. As they wanted to get that productivity gain, a complete quality test needed to start the next day and guess whom they assigned to lead it? A few external auditors temporarily supported me to get as much item coverage across as many stores as possible. I also needed support from the IT department to build a program to align items the regular auditors found in their paper and pencil audits versus our terminal audits. The alignment would help conclude the internal coding accuracy by using the paper and pencil input as the 100% benchmark for accuracy.

Three months later, I was back in the boardroom, presenting the findings from the quality test. As with the productivity test, I went over and above. I showed the quality level to be unacceptable for Nielsen standards. I concluded that the company shouldn't implement the terminals until thoroughly cleansing, item by item, the Cross-Coding Database (CCDB). The "over and above" piece was defining approximately 23 ways that errors were happening. Plus, identifying steps to eliminate or reduce these errors in the future.

It was like déjà vu all over again! Everyone in the room agreed with my conclusion, decided that a cleansing needed to start the next day and guess whom they assigned to lead it?

With more help from the IT department, an auditor, and a coder, in the next three months, we went through every single item on the CCDB – tens of thousands of them! We did so by using a routine I called "The M.A.D. Method." (I also could have called it "The D.A.M. Method," but didn't want to give people the chance to refer to it as "Marty's damn project"). The name's logic was that if you knew the coding was wrong and knew where it should go, you Moved it. If you knew the coding was correct, you Approved it. If you knew the coding was wrong but didn't know where to code it, you would Delete it. If a deleted item was legitimate, it would be re-evaluated by a coder when it came back into the system. The delete step helped clean off hundreds of UPC's that were garbage numbers and not legitimate codes.

Six months of my career, then, were due to curiosity. The initial productivity test mandate did not require any assessment of quality. However, had I not done this out of curiosity, it could have been quite disastrous for the company, given the initial level of quality. I'm sure that something would have happened in another kind of review by someone else before any data would have reached a client, but it would have lost us months this way.

To close this little story, I'm pleased to share that while Canada was the first country to implement this equipment back in the early '80s, Nielsen was still rolling it out into other countries worldwide in the 2010s!

Some years later, I was providing more value to the company by thinking outside my department. Our responsibility was to get new UPC bar codes from manufacturers and conduct several tests to confirm that the printed bars met Canadian retail standards. We had special equipment for doing the measurements and strict steps to follow. After testing, all packages were either returned to the manufacturer or destroyed. Thinking outside the department, I realized that these packages would be invaluable to two other business areas. First, they would help the Coding department. Getting the actual package would ensure that the product got into the system with all the right characteristics. The other department was responsible for taking pictures and measurements of products included in Nielsen's space management solution. As with Coding, this allowed us to get all the right information into the system before the item details were received from a retailer, making it more efficient. After both departments finished, the packages were returned to my team for final handling as per the usual procedure.

As you can see, thinking outside my department created an efficiency and quality benefit to two others. I did realize, though, that this was going to be the extent of innovation or change. That is the thought that prompted me to look at an internal job posting for a junior developer position in another department. The role was to use proprietary software to build category management reports for our retailer and manufacturer clients. You're probably wondering, "Why would he consider going from a leadership role to a junior, individual contributor role, which looks like a demotion?" That's a very valid question.

In my mind, the department I was leading had a precise and narrow mandate. There was no need or expectation for it to change as it served a full and necessary purpose. By undertaking self-reflection, I knew the current role would become boring soon. In comparison, the junior role would require on-going creativity and would <u>add</u> a client-facing element to my experiences. Adding experience is related to Kaizen in terms of continuous improvement! You will hear more about this role later. Suffice it to say, it was a springboard to an ex-pat assignment in the UK. If you'd like to know more about that time in my career, I've written a book, also available on Amazon, called "You Packed A Screwdriver? Our Expat Adventure to Europe and Beyond." Check it out! You'll see more examples of the things I'm sharing in this book, which you can learn and leverage for your benefit.

Later, I worked in a sales and service role, which bookended my career. Having started at the company by collecting the market research data, then moving into Operations departments, afterwards an IT-type group and now selling solutions into the client covered the lot! Within Operations, things evolved, and at one point, I led a team of 30 associates spread across ten countries in Europe and the Americas. A role like this stretches you further and forces you to think in different ways. Particularly when you must lead a team of people, some of whom you will never meet in person, only see over a video call. It also gives you the blessing of making the world much smaller. You get immersed deeply in today's buzzwords of "inclusion and diversity" by having to work with many people who are different culturally and in other ways.

One final story to share as it relates to the mindset you need. I was very blessed over the last three years to have developed a great friendship with Pat Stapleton. Pat played professional ice hockey in the National Hockey League and the World Hockey Association (WHA). His success in the WHA resulted in his induction into their Hall of Fame. He was named to a few all-star teams and was in the running for top defenceman awards. He still holds records in both the NHL and WHA. At times he was named team captain and was the first professional coach for two all-time great hockey legends; Wayne Gretzky and Mark Messier. Pat won many championships at different levels throughout his career. However, his shining moment was playing for the very first Team Canada in the historic 1972 Summit Series against the Soviet Union.

These were terrific accomplishments, at the highest levels of hockey, for someone considered too small. as Pat only stood 5'8" but what made him successful, and what I saw years after his career ended, was his mindset. He lived with and shared this mindset every single day. He always had a "can do" attitude and spoke of having an "attitude of gratitude." He always made me smile with his answer to "How are you today, Pat?" He'd say, "I'm perfect because you're in my life."

Pat and I visited a few grade schools in the Niagara region of Ontario, Canada, to see the results of the initial introduction of a teamwork program. Team Canada was driving this program's development to share what they learned about teamwork back in 1972. Yes, that was years ago, but the lessons learned then are still valid today and will continue to be so into the future. In speaking with the children, Pat was continually giving them mindset messages. He was looking to lay that foundation to help the children on-going. They believed him because he was living proof of the incredible things you can accomplish with the right mindset. Very sadly, on April 8, 2020, Pat passed away. He's gone, but the memory of his messages will stay with me forever.

To get ready for what you're about to learn, it's essential to:

- Have the necessary mindset, which includes Kaisersc plus growth plus positivity.
- Be willing to work at absorbing this information even if it takes a while (perseverance).
- Understand that you will be able to employ the content right out of this book, but if you want to go much deeper into any topic, there are many "single topics" books out there that can give you volumes of detail if necessary.

I'm going to share with you something I do when reading self-development books. You may do this already, but if not, give it some thought. When something specific speaks to me, I highlight or underline that sentence or paragraph. When I finish reading the book, the next step is to go through it again and type up all the highlighted/underlined content. A final step is to go through the typed content and condense it down to a 3-page synopsis. This final condensing makes it easy to revisit these books working in reverse. First, I read the synopsis, and if more detail is necessary, I go to the other typed document. If even more is required, I can then go back to the book itself. We're all swamped, so this makes it easy to refresh our minds on information that provides value to us.

Finally, later, I also talk about reciprocity. And while you have allowed me to earn a few dollars by purchasing this book, I hope you go the extra mile in two ways. Firstly, please send me a note on how you've received value from its teachings. I also want you to let me know every time the content helps you. Did it get you a new job or opportunity, a promotion, a nice raise…? And when the book first helps you, let your friends and colleagues know. It's essential to want others to succeed and to celebrate their success. It's a leadership quality and a vital element of a positive mindset. There is plenty of success to go around for everyone; we don't need to hoard it for ourselves. We need to create a win-win environment!

CHAPTER 2

UNDERSTANDING THE CONTENTS' IMPACT ON YOU

Much of the content in this book will be new knowledge on different topics. However, in an overarching sense, the book will also need you to implement and have a continuous awareness of the necessary mindset. In the previous chapter, I introduced you to "Kaisersc" and mentioned a "positive" attitude. These two things align with a term you may have heard previously - a growth mindset. Psychologist Carol Dweck and colleagues conceived that term. Thinking in this way is a process to improve your capabilities over time. To me, this sounds like an American version of Kaizen. One of the real positives of a growth mindset is that "challenges or failures are viewed as opportunities to grow" rather than a sign that you're inadequate. Another valuable positive is that this mindset gives you a hunger for learning, which is extremely critical for growth, leadership, and continuous improvement. It's interesting to see that "eager to learn or know something" is the definition of curiosity!

To help you understand why this book is essential in your career, let's talk about the 9-Box Matrix. We used this tool in the latter part of my corporate work. It continues to be used in many corporations today. Even if it isn't formally used in companies, no matter how big or small, the thinking is certainly there, even if some of it is in the sub-conscious. If that is the case where you work, keep this visual and concept in mind as it will informally come into play.

9-Box Matrix

So, what is the 9-Box Matrix? This tools' leading utility is in succession planning, vitally important to a company's long-term success. We used it twice a year during talent reviews. The first review helped determine any surprises, either positive or negative, since the last review. It was also the first chance to discuss any newcomers to the team. At year-end, the second review was more critical in many ways because it tied in closely with the recommendations for promotions and salary increases.

While the concept is the same, you may find examples online where the box's labels differ. To illustrate that fact, I made up the labels in the matrix on the next page.

	LOW	MODERATE	HIGH
HIGH (Potential)	Future Star	Looming Star	Consistent Star
MODERATE (Potential)	Inconsistent	Core Player	Key Player
LOW (Potential)	Risk	Mediocre	Constant

PERFORMANCE →

Before we go further in this book, I'd like to highlight something else that's very important. You will often hear the terms management and leadership. Most people think the terms are the same, completely interchangeable. I, however, believe that they are distinctly different. For me, management is related to "things," and leadership adds the element of "people." Now, I hope this does not confuse things for you, but "leaders also need to manage." Leaders manage things but think and act in terms of their impact on people.

I'm going to talk more about this near the end of the book. The reason being I know that many of you will become leaders of others someday. What I want, though, is for you to become leaders and not what I term a manager, or even worse, "manager by default." If you bought this book and later come to realize that you're currently a "manager by default," I hope it raises an awareness that helps you make the changes you need to make to drive greater success for your team and business. As there are three types (leader, manager,

manager by default), and they are distinctly different, for the most part, in this book, I will use the generic word "boss" unless I specifically need to use one of the other terms.

Now, back to the 9-Box Matrix! As you read through the rest of this section, you will understand why I think we can relate what professional poker players do, in opponent assessments and their self-assessment, to what happens at work.

All leadership peers were invited to join the review call simultaneously, which certainly added an engaging element. In this way, you had your boss and your peers at times, challenging you as to why certain people were in specific boxes. It wasn't usually the lower boxes where you would be challenged, but the higher ones. At times I would provide this "challenge feedback" to the individual on my team if it was warranted. For the most part, the feedback was really that the individual was not doing enough to make themselves and their contributions more visible to people outside my team. I would take steps to give people visibility in department meetings and sometimes on the weekly leadership call. However, and here's a tip, the individual should be looking at what they can do themselves to increase visibility. Examples were offering to share ideas or innovations or client experiences on department calls, volunteering for special projects or additional tasks, or leading one of our community groups.

It's only a few pages later, but at this point, I want to remind you of a critical element that you should commit to memory. While it is a boss's responsibility to support your efforts to develop your career – it is your responsibility to drive your career. You know where you want to go and need to figure out how to get there. It would be best to communicate this clearly to your boss, so they know how to support you. If your career is as the owner of a business, you know it's your responsibility to drive your business. All the advice in this book will apply even more if you have employees. Hopefully, you impact them as a leader and not one of the other two options!

The nice thing about the 'all peer call' is that it allowed our boss to validate people's placements, comparing them across teams. This step helps to deal with peers who overvalue their people and rate them too high because they don't want to have the difficult conversations required by lower ratings. While I needed to ensure meritocracy within my team, our group leader needed to ensure meritocracy across the group. This step would prevent a peer from recognizing and rewarding someone on their team as a 'Consistent Star' when they weren't more capable or had more potential than someone on my team whom I placed as a 'Key Player.'

After everyone in the department is bucketed in the matrix, you do a final sense check. You want to ensure that all staff have been fairly placed. Typically, you will get a few people on the high potential row, a few on the low potential row and most of them in the moderate potential/moderate performance box. The matrix would then look like the illustration on the next page (the letters represent separate people).

		Future Star A	Looming Star F	Consistent Star J
POTENTIAL	**HIGH**			
	MODERATE	Inconsistent	Core Player C, E, G, I	Key Player D
	LOW	Risk B	Mediocre	Constant H
		LOW	MODERATE	HIGH

PERFORMANCE →

The next step, then, is questions around people in specific boxes. For the employees in the 'Consistent Star' box, you discuss if you should promote them. If they were in that box at the mid-year point, there's a good chance a promotion now makes sense. If they have just moved into that box during this review, then the promotion could be six months down the road unless now is the right timing. For those in the 'Looming Star' box, you may discuss what needs to be worked on to improve their performance so they can move to the 'Consistent Star' box. A similar conversation is held on the 'Future Star' box to see what needs to be done next year to move them across the matrix. For advancement and succession, it's only those people that are on the "high potential" row that come into the conversation. So, make sure you are doing what you can to be on that row!

Of course, there's always the other side of the coin. Here we're talking about those on the low potential row who are also low to moderate performers. There are only one of two questions the group leader asks if you're in these two boxes. The best one is, "Do you have a development plan in place to improve this persons' performance?" The alternative question is, "When are you going to exit them from the business?"

Some people are in these boxes as they have no passion for what they're doing or don't work hard as they have a negative predisposition. This condition may result from them thinking things aren't fair or they aren't being recognized for their work. These are external views when they should be doing some self-reflection to see if the problem lies within them. These people would benefit significantly from this book.

Other times people are in these boxes because of operational and role changes forced upon them. I had a situation like this a few years ago upon moving into a new department and inheriting an existing team. Within six weeks, I realized that two people on the team were in the lower two boxes. As opposed to the previous statements, they did have a passion for work and did not have a negative predisposition. So, what was the problem then? They had worked for several years in purely operational roles. Then one day, they were informed that organizational changes were occurring, and they had two choices. The first choice was to move into new positions that included some 'client-facing' elements, which, in truth, neither wanted. The second choice was to lose their jobs. As you can tell, they both decided to stay with the company. I couldn't work with them very closely as they were in another country. This geographic difference meant it would take extra time to answer the question as to whether specific training and coaching could help them improve their performance to at least the Core Player box. If an improvement couldn't be accomplished, then the next step would be to exit them.

A company cannot afford to carry people in the lowest row for too long.

Some weeks later, I travelled to their office to give them the unfortunate news face-to-face. I felt that as they were long-term employees, admirable individuals and tried hard, they deserved the personal approach rather than a phone call. In my conversation with Susan (not her real name), she did not express any surprise at the decision. We discussed how this could turn out positive as I knew she was still working to keep herself occupied as her husband was away for a significant time on his job. My next conversation with Hal (not his real name) was the most difficult I've ever had in giving someone this news. I'd never had difficulty exiting people due to poor performance because of unacceptable actions or attitudes or even things like theft. However, in this case, there was Hal, who was a wonderful person. In the perfect job for him, you'd want Hal on your team. As a person, you'd like him as a neighbour. I was almost in tears giving him the bad news. What made it even worse was that he completely understood and certainly wasn't questioning or challenging me on the decision.

After those two conversations, I had the rest of the team come into a separate meeting to let them know the decision. It was a little uncomfortable because Susan's sister was also on the team and sitting next to me during this announcement. A few times in the following weeks, I enquired on how Susan was doing. The last answer was, "She's delighted being home full-time now; this is the best thing that could have happened." I had assumed that answer based on conversations I'd had with Susan over the weeks, but it was fantastic to have it confirmed by her sister. Hal eventually found another job that didn't have the stress of doing something he didn't want to do. I was very happy for him as well.

Here, we have identified the top people for whom there will be promotions or unique opportunities soon. We've also determined the bottom people who need a development plan or to be removed. Most everyone else is the majority core of your team. The first step in meritocracy is placing people in the matrix fairly across the team. The next one is then ranking the people within your group. While the placement of people in boxes will have a considerable differentiation between your 'stars' and your 'risks,' this step has a more granular, more impactful differentiation. The reason being you may have ten people on your team, and four of them are in the same box. In ranking them, you can't have all four with the same rank, so you need to look at what small things differentiate them. The illustration below shows where people are in the boxes and how they subsequently are ranked:

POTENTIAL	LOW	MODERATE	HIGH
HIGH	Future Star A	Looming Star F	Consistent Star J
MODERATE	Inconsistent	Core Player C, E, G, I	Key Player D
LOW	Risk B	Mediocre	Constant H

PERFORMANCE →

RANK	EMPLOYEE
1	J
2	D
3	F
4	E
5	C
6	I
7	G
8	H
9	A
10	B

You may look at this and wonder why person 'D,' with moderate potential, is ranked ahead of person 'F' with High Potential. The same question can come with how you compare persons 'A' and 'H.' The decision, for me, is around what they are delivering today versus their potential to generate in the future. Remember, one of the main reasons for the matrix is succession planning.

The ranking will then come into play when deciding things like bonus payments and salary increases. An example of how this could look is:

Employee	9-Box	Rank	Increase %
J	Consistent Star	1	6.0
D	Key Player	2	4.2
F	Looming Star	3	3.8
E	Core Player	4	3.4
C	"	5	3.1
I	"	6	3.1
G	"	7	3.0
H	Constant	8	2.6
A	Future Star	9	2.5
B	Risk	10	1.0

If you think of yourself as one of the many 'Core Players,' do you want the 4th or 7th ranked increase? You need to differentiate yourself from others!

The dictionary defines meritocracy as "A society governed by people selected according to merit." In placing people in the 9-Box Matrix, then ranking them, then determining their salary or bonus increases, you make decisions based on meritocracy. Hopefully, you do this with no unconscious bias at play. (You'll read more about this bias later in the book.)

It's essential for employees to understand meritocracy, how it works and unfolds. However, some of them will not get it, and I hope that's never you. I'll share an actual example based on someone who reported to me. At the end of his annual performance review, he said, "Can I ask you a question?" I said, "Sure." He then asked, "I think I should be promoted to a Senior position; can you do that for me?" As I had just given him a "Meets Expectations" rating, I wondered why he would think that should result in a promotion, so I asked why. His response was, "Other people have been promoted to Senior this year, and I've been on the job longer than them." I quickly explained that the length of service had nothing to do with promotions. Moving to a Senior level meant that he had to shine over and above almost every junior, which is what meritocracy was all about.

As I've mentioned before, it is the individual's responsibility to drive their career, but as his leader, it was my responsibility to support this goal wherever possible. So, I told him that one way to shine above the others was to step up and take a leadership role in one of the departments' communities. When he did this, I would support him by ensuring he got onto one or two of our weekly leadership calls to share what his community was doing. These calls would give him the much-needed visibility with that group. I also highlighted that this would not be enough on its' own as others were also leading communities. However, it would at least give him some exposure to the leadership team, who would have to support my proposal to promote him down the road. I asked if he understood what he needed to do, and the reply was, "Yes."

A year later, we did his annual review; he achieved 'Meets Expectations' and again asked about getting a promotion. I knew this would be a brief conversation. All I had to ask was, "Did you step up and lead a community, as I recommended?" His answer (which I already knew) was "No." My next and final question was, "Why do you think I would put you up for promotion when you took no action on my key piece of advice?" It looks like he just moved from the 'Core Player' box to the 'Constant' box.

To leverage this chapter, put reminders in your calendar throughout the year to ask yourself two questions. Within which box do you think your boss currently has you placed? What do you need to do to move to a better box (unless you're in the top right corner and can ask about a promotion)? If you can't answer the first question, then have a conversation with your boss. If you can answer the first, but not the second, you can have a different conversation with your boss. Having an awareness of the 9-Box and planning to as those two questions regularly will help you in that area. How about starting right now with your first exercise, which is to answer those two questions.

If you own a business and have employees but don't currently use this tool, stop at this point, and complete the 9-Box Matrix exercise on them. Please place them in the appropriate box, then rank them from top to bottom. Then you can ask yourself several questions such as:

1. Would everyone be aware of which box they are in?
2. Do the people in the bottom left area have development plans designed to help move them up? Or should they be removed?
3. Should you be looking to give additional responsibilities or promote people in the top right boxes?
4. Based on their placement and ranking, are all employees compensated fairly?

After completing this exercise, you should then sit down with each person individually and take them through their placement and what's next, be it a promotion, unique project, or set-up of a development plan.

CHAPTER 3

HOW TO IMPROVE YOUR CHANCES FOR SUCCESS

Differentiation

In everything you do, it's about differentiating yourself from the competition, even if they are your friends. First, let me highlight that differentiation is not the same as diversity, which is a word we hear every day. (By the way, I'm a major supporter of diversity, and it's covered in a later chapter along with unconscious bias.) It's understandable to confuse these two terms as forms of the word "differ" are included in the definition of each. You'll also see "people" included in both. Differentiation is "The action or process of differentiating or distinguishing between two or more things or people." Whereas diversity is defined as "The practice or quality of including or involving people from a range of different social and ethnic backgrounds and of different genders, sexual orientations, etc...."

You always need to be aware of differentiation and its' importance to you and your business. To determine differentiation, you must analyze and understand your competition and, just as important, self-reflect on your skills, knowledge, and experience. Here we are going back to poker again, studying your opponent and yourself. On-going self-refection is a must for many things, including personal growth and being a leader. However, it's not the only part of the full reflection plan you need for yourself, which we will also discuss later.

To help you understand differentiation and how it differs from diversity, think of grocery shopping. Differentiation comes into play when deciding between similar products, much like your clients differentiate when determining which vendor to choose. If you are very loyal to a brand or your client is very dedicated to you, differentiation may not come into play that much. However, the lower the level of loyalty, the more impactful the role of differentiation plays.

Here's a grocery shopping example to help illustrate this point. Let's say you are not dedicated to any specific coffee brand and want to try something different. You go to the store, and there are dozens of potential choices on the shelf in front of you. You don't like instant coffee, which eliminates about a quarter of the options right off the bat. You prefer coffee made with Colombian beans rather than from any other country, reducing the list further. You prefer medium versus dark roast, which eliminates even more items. Next, you reduce choices down to those brands you know can be trusted. With the few products in play, you see that the larger sizes are more cost-effective than the smaller ones. With even fewer items left in the game and their equal prices, it can now come down to the packaging. You pick the one whose packaging has caught your eye, and off you go. Some weeks later, you come back to the store and this time see that one of the coffees you almost picked last time is now on sale, and this differentiation makes you buy it this time around.

Just for fun, the next time you go grocery shopping, look to see how often differentiation comes into play in your final buying decision. Always keep in mind that differentiation means perhaps *just that one key thing* that makes people or companies pick you!

If you've applied for or will be applying for a new job, here's another exercise you can do now. Answer this question, "What would differentiate you from other applicants that have the same skill set and experience as you?" If you're not applying for a job but hoping for a promotion soon, who would your competition be? When you determine that, what would differentiate you from them for the decision to go your way? If you can't answer those questions at this point, that's okay. Working through the book will give you some other exercises and ideas to help form an answer. The most important thing is that you are aware that you need to answer the differentiation question for your benefit.

Skill Set Matrix

In this section, we'll look at a tool you can use for self-reflection when applying for a new role. I'm using the term Skill Set Matrix (SSM) here, but you may find others using Skills Matrix or Skills Matrices. They're all the same thing. In basic terms, an SSM is an organized way in which to see skills and qualifications across a wide range of employees. It is mainly utilized when looking at an operational process or when setting up short-term projects. The main objective is to ensure that the team members have all the required skills, to the needed level of expertise, for the process or project. However, I've used the tool in other ways, such as:

- Identifying development plan needs for the current role or career growth
- Identifying training sources for said plan
- Tracking development completion
- Use for self-reflection when applying for a new position

Okay, these other uses aren't from the traditional way, so I'll share some stories to convey why I listed these utilities.

Career Examples

These examples are from my career in which the SSM came, or should have come, into play. From a leader's perspective, the matrix confirms if they have the right amount of people with all the skills needed to keep the process running. Otherwise, you could run into problems if the only person that had a particular skill decided to leave the company with two weeks' notice. Or, in the case of Nielsen, the company unknowingly created the situation on their own. For some years, the Nielsen Company has been proactively downsizing employees. One day, a senior leader in the Canadian company found out that the IT person assigned to build web solutions for her had their position eliminated. In the next senior executive meeting, she highlighted that her department was charged with several objectives to drive revenue and improve relationships with its retailer partners. However, the ONLY person in the building with the necessary web skills was being downsized! The next day the IT employee was called into HR and asked if he would like to keep his job. At the time this was a positive turn of events for him given other things going on. So, he remained, built the solutions, and helped the senior leaders' department achieve their goals. Situations can be that precarious if you don't have a clear view of the skills needed and whether you have them covered or not.

There are different ways to set up or utilize a matrix. You can create one for a single role across which you can compare multiple people. Or you can create a matrix with various functions to view the strength of a team. There are even different ways of assessing people. You could identify if they have that skill, yes or no, or you could enter a rating. The rating could be a range of 0 to 3, with 0 representing 'does not have the skill or knowledge' to 3 being at a 'master-level' where they should train others. You could also enter a percent with the range going from 0 to 100. Or you could come up with something else that makes sense to you.

In the rows, we had several items listed under the headings of Hard Skills, Soft Skills, and Industry Knowledge. We used a rating system to identify if their expertise/knowledge level was None, Basic, Intermediate or Master. We did expect there to be different ratings for people in the same role. For example, with Industry Knowledge, we expected people from another Nielsen department to be a Master level for all items. Then, you could expect "None" for the level of expertise/knowledge with external recruits. These would typically be recent graduates. Then, in the columns, we recorded all the different roles in the department. On this master matrix, we indicated the skill level needed for each position.

In setting up a new team in Mexico City, I copied the master SSM (Excel-based) and removed all roles except theirs. Then, on these personal assessment sheets, I changed each of the ratings (None, Basic, Intermediate and Master) into numerical ratings (0, 1, 2 and 3). There was one column with the desired rating, and in the next column, each person entered their estimated rating. I had also added a third column to calculate the difference between the two. On this column, I placed Excel conditional formatting to colour code any difference that was positive (green) or negative (red). The next column had links or verbiage to find training material or class schedules to place into their development plan. Training would be a requirement for any difference that was colour coded red due to a negative score. Then there were columns to plan target dates for any training plus enter the completion date. These columns would help them stay on track. Forwarding the file on a bi-weekly basis allowed me to assess their training progress quickly.

Having a master Skill Set Matrix across multiple jobs supported conversations around career planning. For example, we had progressive roles of Global Client Liaison (GCL), Senior Global Client Liaison and various Leader positions. For leadership skills, the expected rating was None for GCL, Intermediate for Senior GCL and Master for the Leader titles. That meant that if a GCL intended to move to Senior, we would work with them to develop an intermediate leadership level. If a Senior wanted to move to a Leader role, there would be much more intensive training required to move them from Intermediate to Master. These two points are a simple but impactful example of a way to use an SSM to drive your career!

After Nielsen, I started teaching at Fanshawe College and used the SSM process as an exercise with my students. They needed to be organized into teams for group work on a case study to be written, then presented to the class. There are different ways that professors create groups. Some deal a deck of cards; everyone with an Ace is on one team, Kings on another. Some group people together in alphabetical order of their last names. Some let the students decide, which usually means they quickly scramble to pick their friends. I wanted the students to experience how an SSM could be used to select the best possible team. I created a worksheet in Excel with everyone's names in the rows and the eight skills necessary for success in the columns. Some of the skills listed were analytical ability, detail orientation, and creativity. The instructions for the students to complete their analysis and make their personnel selections were:

1. On the row containing your name, record a 1 if you have the skill at the top of the column
2. Introduce yourself to every other student in the class and share which skills you have identified as a 1
3. Then, on the row containing their name, record a 1 for the skills every other student claim to possess
4. After you have met with everyone, please give me your top 5 choices for whom you want on the team. List them in your priority order as each team will only be comprised of three people

When they finished, I took all their worksheets to finalize the teams as I expected there to be much duplication in selections of the most skilled students. At the next class, where I shared who was on each team, I also shared my observations of their choices. It was apparent that some did not understand the concept, while others still picked friends, creating a weaker team. I felt this was the case by observing:

1. Two students with the most skills were not picked <u>at all</u> by seven people
2. One of those two people was not a first or second choice of <u>anyone</u>
3. One person with the second-lowest number of skills was chosen by 64% of the group
4. Two people didn't get any of their Top 5 picks. There were better fits that they did not include in their Top 5 <u>at all</u>. I placed the better fits on their team to improve their chances of a higher grade

For interest's sake, or if you were curious, problem solving, and teamwork were skills identified as being possessed by 83% of the class. On the other side of the coin, only 42% of the students thought they had negotiating skills, and only 33% had an analytical ability. If every student possessed every skill, the total class score would be 100%. With this class, the total score was 58%. So, lots of room and need for skill development! This exercise was a great way to teach them things like making leadership type decisions (pick skills over friends), building strong teams, and self-reflection. Hopefully, they have learned from this exercise and will implement some of the things I'm going to discuss next.

SSM Process for Job Posting

In some ways, you are using the SSM process when you are searching for a job. How is that? Every job has a list of qualifications (skills and knowledge) that the company desires in the ideal candidate. You may be interested in the position, and as you look through the qualifications list, you measure yourself against those needs. The jobs that each reader of this book will be looking for will be quite different. However, the process to work through an assessment will be the same. To explain how this works, lets' look at the example of competencies required by a Business Analyst (BA) role advertised today:

- Completed degree or diploma as Business Analyst
- 2-3 years of demonstrated experience in working across multiple business units and service delivery channels to launch IT system improvements
- Experience coordinating IT system improvements in consultation with individuals from non-technical backgrounds
- Technical knowledge or experience with a customized database with SQL Server experience an asset

- A change-oriented mindset with a passion for continuous improvement and commitment to excellence:

    o Analytical problem solving and time-management skills

    o Ability to handle multiple tasks, priorities and meet deadlines
- Ability to communicate effectively in technical, business and community environments
- Proficiency in database report writing, queries and exports
- Expert level proficiency with Microsoft Office (MS Access)
- Experience working with not-for-profit organizations that have multiple funding envelopes an asset

I selected this job posting example to highlight that companies are looking for some of the soft skills covered in this book. The examples here are a change-oriented mindset, passion for continuous improvement, analytical problem solving (Six Sigma), time-management skills and meeting deadlines (project planning). Just in case you aren't aware of the difference, hard skills lend themselves more to quantification. Examples are someone's computer programming ability, a degree, or the ability to operate specific machinery. Soft skills are communications and relationships, which are not easily quantified, but we still need to rate our capability in these areas.

This job posting can be viewed for different purposes by different people. One person could be in a position, experience-wise, to apply for the job today. However, a student who will graduate this year with a Business Analyst degree or someone just starting to work in this area will look at it for guidance on which skills they need to develop over the next few years.

For the person wanting to apply to the BA opening today, the first step is self-reflection to match their skills and experience to those required plus the mastery level. For example, they are looking for an <u>expert level</u> proficiency with Microsoft Access. Should they feel they match up well with the requirements, the next steps are around their resume, cover letter, SOAR stories and interview prep.

For people considering this job for the future, self-reflection will determine their gap against the required skills and mastery level. For example, with Access, they are only at a beginner or intermediate level, meaning there's currently a gap. They should then craft a 1 to 2-year development plan to address the gaps.

Using the SSM at Work

After you complete the Skill Set Matrix, your boss should confirm your rating as accurate if they know you well enough. This step is the same as an annual performance review, where you both rate performance and align on a final number. Your boss's rating is essential to gain a more accurate measure to set an optimum development plan. For example, you may think you're great at a particular skill, but your boss can make a valid comparison with your peers and knows that you are okay, not excellent. Rating yourself on your own, you wouldn't put anything into a development plan for this skill. However, from the boss's perspective, you would include it in the plan, which is better for you in the long run. Conversely, some people will undervalue some of their abilities, thinking they need to improve when, in fact, they are excellent. They can then allocate training/study time elsewhere for a better benefit.

If you are managing people, look to get all the relevant external input called 360-degree feedback. It's 360-degrees as the information is from you, your boss, peers, and direct reports. The value of getting evaluations from these other groups is that they work with you in different ways and, typically, on divergent tasks or topics. Therefore, they will bring very different perspectives to your skills. Another value of feedback from others is, as mentioned before, they can identify your "blind spots." These are areas of skills or characteristics that are lacking or hurting you somehow, and you don't realize it. If you're not currently a leader with direct reports, you could look for internal clients' feedback instead. If you're not presently working, look for feedback from a previous boss or peers, a mentor or valued friends who can be objective. Anyone who knows you well enough to rate your skills accurately. By the way, this is something you should be doing for your annual performance review at a minimum.

Keep this in mind as well. After completing your skill set rating, congratulate yourself for all those where you rate highly. Use this as a confidence booster to feel good about yourself, especially if you're not currently working. Unemployment can be a challenging time in our lives. We can feel negative, depressed, and hopeless. I know, I've been there! So, we certainly need to feel upbeat about something, anything. Besides that, to get out of unemployment means winning at a job interview. Your chances of success there are increased if you project the image that you feel good about yourself. Use this rating exercise to build confidence and start that positive mindset, so it comes through in your interviews. Then for those skills you place in a development plan, instead of being disappointed, be pleased you now have a plan to improve, bringing more significant benefit to you and your future.

The Tool for You

There is more to say about how a leader or company can use and adjust a Skill Set Matrix, but I'm not going to go into that detail here. Why not? The purpose of this book is to focus on bringing you more insights on what you should know to drive great success for yourself. Besides that, you should understand the SSM process even if your company doesn't use one. We're going to look at this as creating an on-going tool for you to personally use no matter what job or company or industry you will move into over your career. It will be a valuable tool to use in your development planning.

I recommend that you follow the same process for the remainder of your career, any time you want to make a change. Even if that change is moving from working for someone to working for yourself, what are all the skills required in your entrepreneurship and do you need to add them, improve them, or outsource the work? If you're already a business owner, is this something you should implement across all your staff to see where they need to improve? The SSM is a great tool to use as part of career path discussions with your team. Where can they go from their current role, and what skills and skill levels do they need? How do they stack up against the need, and what can they do to fill any gaps? Embrace it as a vital tool for continued self-improvement for driving your career!

An exercise you can undertake now is to look at the next job for your career journey. Find an appropriate job posting and, in Excel, write down all the hard skills, soft skills and industry knowledge that the job requires. Then, make some assumptions as to the level of expertise needed for each. You will have some clues in the job posting where they say "expert" or "intermediate" or "some knowledge."

If you're working and the job is internal, a great idea is asking the hiring manager what rating they would look for on each skill. They may be impressed that you're going through this kind of reflection and development planning! For students or those currently out of work, this can be a part of a networking conversation. Who knows, it may help you be discovered by someone new as a potential hire! If these conversations are not possible, and where you are in doubt, it's best to assume the required level to be intermediate or master. Rate yourself for each of these, then get one or more people to sense-check your estimate. When you're happy with your ratings, calculate the differences. Be satisfied where your score equals or exceeds the job requirements.

For those items where your score is less than desired, look at what kind of training you could do to improve those areas. When you know what needs to be accomplished, identify completion dates. After you finish this training, you will be well-positioned to move into that role in the future. Keep in mind, as I mentioned earlier, this process can be used for any job, in any company, in any industry. Not only that, but you can also use this process over and over throughout your career.

SMART Goals

I'd now like to share with you SMART Goals if you've not heard of this tool. We all create several goals over the lifetime of our careers. Most often, they are set in your annual performance review or for assigned projects. I would assume, as well, that you also create many goals in your personal life, be they at home or for any charity work you may do.

How well have you done hitting your goals over the years? Have you done better hitting them at work or home? If there's been a difference, why is that? I've done a better job hitting them at work rather than at home. I know, for sure, that my wife will vouch for that statement!

There are many reasons for people not hitting their goals, and here are a few of the main ones:

1. They don't even set goals in the first place. Yes, you can argue that they couldn't miss something they didn't set. However, in your mind moving forward, you must realize that there are always natural or essential goals, whether you establish them or not.
2. They set them, then ignore how they are tracking towards them, like writing goals for an annual performance review and not checking them until you must write your year-end summary.
3. There is little incentive or motivation to complete poorly written goals.

Let's look at each of the above and determine how you're going to address them moving forward:

1. For anything critical for your success, you're going to write a goal!
2. Once you write the goal, you'll determine a process to achieve it successfully. Make sure the method includes a way to track the progress towards completion. As a tip, you can put appointments into your calendar to pop up as a reminder to check progress.
3. Replace poorly written goals with SMART ones!

SMART is a brilliant acronym that makes it easy to remember. Be aware, though, that there are two letters, A and T, where you may see different words used. Some people use Attainable and Timely, instead of what I use, which is on the next page:

S = Specific
M = Measurable
A = Achievable
R = Relevant
T = Timebound

Let's look, in more detail, at each of the components:

S = Specific = A very focused goal with an idea of how you will accomplish it.

M = Measurable = A metric to make the goal impactful and to help you track progress over time. This aids in determining when you've been successful plus the extent of your success.

A = Achievable = This element is a sense check on whether there are any risks or mitigating factors that will make it very difficult or impossible to complete. If this is the case, then you need to determine how to eliminate those factors. If you cannot do this, then perhaps the Measurable metrics or scope of the goal needs to be changed, so you're not set up to fail.

R = Relevant = Is this goal something that's closely related to the impactful needs of what you or your team or department must accomplish? For example, would an objective of learning to play guitar by year-end help your team? This element should identify the real benefit of achieving the goal, which also helps provide a bigger picture context. Thinking in terms of relevance is something very successful people consider when asked to do something. They ask themselves, "Will doing this help me achieve my key goals?" If the answer is no, meaning it's not relevant to their key goals, then they reply "No."

T = Timebound = You must have a deadline associated with the goal and perhaps even incremental milestones identified. If you don't define a finish line, you may deprioritize the task, as there is no sense of urgency.

At times people are too general with their goals. I've seen examples like "I'm going to self-develop this year." Or "I'm going to improve my productivity." With simple statements like that, how would you know if you've been truly successful in the end?

Let's compare how you would write the "self-develop" goal in the SMART way to see the impactful difference. In SMART form, it would now be "I'm going to develop my skills in the area of client relationships by completing one effective listening course plus reading one related book by April 30." Can you see the part aligning to each letter in the acronym?

Let's say there are two people in the same job at the same company. The first person says they are going to have self-development as a goal this year. The second person has the same plan but formed it in the SMART way of:

Specific (develop skills in client relationships)

Measurable (one training course and one book)

Achievable (easy to incorporate this into their schedule)

Relevant (They're client-facing, and this is to improve client relationships)

Timebound (complete by April 30)

Who do you think is going to be more successful? The SMART person will be utilizing these new skills with clients **by May**. Would it be unreasonable to assume the first person hasn't even started their development by then, seeing as they have no deadline to work towards? This action planning is the 'differentiation' between the two. If you had to hire or promote one of these people, who would you pick?

There are a few other actions you also need to take in terms of these goals. For starters, you need to put them in writing. It helps you better visualize the goals. Plus, it provides a quick and easy reference to utilize during optimal check-ins on progress. Optimal means that if your deadline is in 12 weeks, you should review progress at the 6-week mark. If the task takes 12 months, you should be checking progress at least at the 3, 6- and 9-month marks. Progress checks are critical to success! You will not believe how many people have reported to me over the years that only check their progress a few days before their annual performance review. There is a distinct correlation between a last-minute check of goals and their careers stalling. Yet usually, they wondered why they weren't going anywhere. It helps to have mini celebrations at each of the review points, especially for long timelines, as they can generate the motivation you need to keep going. Upon completion of the goal, the last action is to *celebrate* your success appropriately.

As I need to practice what I preach, here are two SMART goals for myself with regards to this book:

"I will write a book, of at least 190 pages, to share many of the tools, ideas and techniques I use to help individuals who are just starting, or stalled, in their careers or their business; and have the book self-published on Amazon by the end of November 2020."

"I will track the progress the sales of this book weekly and adjust marketing, pricing and advertising on platforms such as Amazon, LinkedIn and Facebook to achieve a minimum sales target of 53,000 units by the end of December 2023."

Let's break each of these goals into the SMART acronym:

Goal #1 – Writing the book

Specific = Write a book to share many of the tools, ideas and techniques I use to help individuals who are just starting or stalled in their careers or business and have the book self-published on Amazon.

Measurable = At least 190 pages.

Achievable = As I started this in late June, this gives me around five months for the multiple drafts I'll write, plus an editor's review plus get the cover professionally created then getting the content into Amazon, so yes, this is achievable!

Relevant = My business card labels me as "Team Leader/Mentor/Coach," so writing a book to help others in their work and life is very much in line.

Timebound = A definite deadline is set as the book needs to be launched by the end of November 2020.

Goal #2 – Book Sales

Specific = I will track the sales of this book and adjust marketing, pricing, and advertising on platforms such as Amazon, LinkedIn and Facebook.

Measurable = Achieve a minimum sales target of 53,000 units.

Achievable = In terms of what is in my control regarding tracking and adjusting, this is undoubtedly achievable. There is a challenge, though, in terms of the sales target as that relies on others. When the value in the content benefits people like you, then perhaps a review gets written on Amazon or Goodreads or BookBub, which encourages other people to buy the book. Or maybe they directly recommend this book to friends, work colleagues and connections. As much as I'm writing this book to help others, I hope the readers will make recommendations to do the same.

Relevant = I'm 100% convinced that the information in this book can help anyone and everyone. As mentioned in goal #1, this is relevant to my Team Leader/Mentor/Coach label.

Timebound = This first instance of time is the weekly progress review, and the second instance is the December 2023 deadline.

As you can see, I now have very structured and focused goals to help successfully steer me over the next 3 ½ years. Now I need to utilize project planning essentials to break these goals down into more digestible and manageable chunks. I'm not a trained PM, and neither will you need be to use the project planning information contained later in chapter 5.

When we're learning something new, it's vital to put it into practice as quickly as possible. That's why I always talk about "Just-in-time training." We're all busy and overloaded with incoming information every waking hour. If we go for too long between learning and using that new information, we forget most of it. Therefore, what I'd like you to do is stop reading this book right now and look at writing at least one business SMART goal for yourself. If there's something you've been struggling with at work, or it seems overwhelming, this will help you focus on accomplishing the task.

As well, why not write one for your personal life? If you're a student or not currently working, then the individual goal is the exercise for you. Perhaps there's something you've wanted to accomplish for quite some time now but haven't got around to it yet. You can even make it something relatively easy to achieve so you can see how SMART works. Please chunk out what part relates to each letter in the acronym when you finish writing the goal. This step ensures that the goal is optimally written.

Through self-reflection, you identified areas in which you needed to improve. Now you have set some SMART goals to help in that area. Self-reflection also had you identify skills or experiences where you are indeed a "Master." In these cases, you can now create SOAR stories that are critical for interviews or promoting yourself.

SOAR Stories

I'm sure that some of you, at this point, are thinking you don't need to read this section as you are not actively searching for a job. While the information is valuable for interviews, it's also beneficial for networking or sales situations. How can that be? Let me share a personal story to illustrate why I make that connection, to help you remember this advice in the future.

Not long ago, I was having lunch with Joe Smith (not his real name), who had been President and CEO of a national brewery, then later Senior VP of Marketing for a North American professional ice hockey team. So, when Joe was talking, I was effectively listening. While working with the brewer, he had some invaluable business deals with companies in other countries. The most insightful aspect was a comment on how Joe achieved agreements with other companies. He didn't bother spending much time selling the product itself because "beer is beer and there are thousands of them." He said, "I didn't sell them on the beer, I sold them on Joe Smith!" Yes, his company's product was well-liked, but there were many other beers out there that were just as good. So, the 'differentiator' would be in what Joe Smith, himself, could bring to the table. This realization tells me that the process you would go through for networking or sales is very similar to what you would go through in an interview. In all instances, it's demonstrating to the other party that you have the right stuff based on past, proven successes. You can make things happen in a positive way for everyone's benefit.

There are many books available on the market that exclusively cover the topic of interviewing. You can find them on Amazon priced anywhere from $10-$79. An interview is integral to your career; it gets you in the door and then moving around within a company. And remember, you're always up against stiff competition. I recommend buying a book exclusively on the topic as it will go into greater detail than I do here. However, as is the concept for this book, I want to give you a decent view and understanding of a wide range of topics and, where you feel it's a necessity, you can buy another book that focuses in more depth on one topic. As mentioned before, I buy books, then highlight items that speak to me, type them up, then condense them to about three pages of notes I can utilize. I'm trying to give you as close to the "three-page view" as possible. Then you can go in the reverse order up to a specific topic book.

The high-level points with interviewing are:

- Knowing your SOAR stories that relate to the job qualifications
- Researching the company to understand their business
- Being prepared with a few key questions *
- Being enthusiastic during the interview
- Sending a post-interview "thank you"

* There are two parts to this point to be discussed later

If you've never heard of the SOAR acronym, it stands for:

S = Situation
O = Obstacles
A = Action
R = Results

Note that you may find some people referring to 'O' as Opportunity. To me, the Situation is the Opportunity, and it's of more value to discuss any Obstacles you had to overcome. It's easy to get results when there are no problems to be faced, so when hiring people, I always looked for ones who had to deal with obstacles.

What, then, is an example of a SOAR story? Let's say that two of the job qualifications were project planning and prioritization. A perfect anecdote, in this case, would be something like this. "I was informed that a major sale had just been made to a new client. There was a problem in that the sales team promised a delivery date, which my team didn't have the capacity to meet. So, I called the team together to discuss their workload schedule. We looked for any work that could be reprioritized plus put a hold on all non-client type work. We also looked at what steps, for the new sale, could be worked concurrently by a few people rather than consecutively by one person. This resulted in hitting the tight timeline for the major sale without disrupting any other client work."

Let's look at each component of the acronym in this story:

Situation = I was informed that client service had just made a major sale to a new client.

Obstacle = There was a problem in that the sales team promised a delivery date, which my team couldn't meet.

Action = I called the team together to discuss their workload and schedule. We looked for any work, particularly non-client, that could be re-prioritized. We also looked at what steps, for the new sale, could be worked concurrently by a few people rather than consecutively by one person.

Results = This resulted in hitting the tight timeline for the major sale without disrupting any other client work.

SOAR is a great model for creating impactful stories to communicate your abilities. Many of these stories should be within your resume as this document needs to show results! They are also handy to share during any networking activity. As they are suitable for networking, you should not wait for a future interview to create your stories. Here's another exercise. Stop at this point and write at least 1 SOAR story that would quantify your biggest strength. Then, look to eventually have ten stories written and ready to share when needed. A by-product of this exercise is that it can give you a source of pride to see, in writing, ten of your key accomplishments.

Here's one final, critical point that I would like to share. These stories do not necessarily have to be work-related. They can be about the obstacles you've overcome in your personal life. Whether the result was at work or in your personal life shouldn't matter. What should matter is the situation and obstacle you faced, the actions you took and the results. It's about clearly demonstrating proven abilities that you will leverage to be successful in the next role. Personal SOAR stories are essential for graduates who may not have had a job to this point. Tip: If the hiring manager doesn't want to hear any SOAR stories accomplished outside of work, this should be a red flag. They cannot think outside the box or recognize that leadership is about people and not just things.

ATS, HR and the Interview

At this point, you have completed self-reflection and training to improve in the areas you needed to develop. You have also identified SOAR stories of where you've been very successful. Now you're ready to start applying for jobs, which is a multi-faceted process. What we'll review here are the three steppingstones with a potential employer.

The first critical step for moving to another job is to have a "connectable" resume. Why do I use the word connectable? These days many individual job postings receive hundreds of applications. This volume means that HR can't possibly go through every application. Even if they did look at each one, they'd only spend around 8 seconds looking for specific words. Therefore, many larger companies are employing an Applicant Tracking System (ATS), referred to as a talent management system. What is essential to know is how the ATS automates the review of all submitted resumes. When you upload your resume online, the ATS puts it into a format to search for keywords. On the plus side, these words are found in the job posting itself. Therefore, you need to have a master resume, which you will custom tweak for every job application. You want to ensure to include all the keywords from the posting into your resume that legitimately apply. You then hope that the ATS review matches up enough words to rate you as a desired candidate. Unfortunately, if it doesn't, then you're instantly ignored and don't make it to the next step.

A few crucial tips here. Firstly, when your resume uploads online, check it carefully to ensure your job titles and descriptions are fully there and in the right places. Depending on your document's layout and how the ATS scans it, the system can load vital information into the wrong boxes. If this happens, you will not get through this step even if you were the most qualified candidate! Trust me, I've seen how much an ATS can completely mess up a resume load. Next, to improve your chances, please make sure that the keywords you use match the job application in the same way. Reason being that different companies can use different terminology for the same skill. For example, you could see client management, account management, and client relations across three job postings. So, if your master resume says, "account management," but the job posting says "client management," change your resume to match as they're the same thing.

Let's say that your resume gets selected by the ATS to move onto the next step, which is HR reviewing your cover letter to whittle down the list of candidates further. Again, there's lots of great advice out there on how to construct a cover letter. In concise terms, the content needs to intrigue them enough to want to have a conversation. You can achieve this by identifying your differentiating value and a compelling insight you have on the company. The latter point is why it's vital to research the company before writing the letter.

If you make it past HR, the next step is the interview (or multiple interviews), where the final decision gets made. The first thing you must realize is that as much as you want the job, the interviewer will decide based on what they want, not what you want. Instead of looking at the interview solely from your perspective, it's more important to look at it from their perspective. One thing to keep in mind, which should help you psychologically, is that the company feels you have merit because <u>they have invited you for an interview</u>. This invitation means they do see something positive in your background and experience. In many ways, then, think of yourself as being halfway to the job, with the remaining task to differentiate yourself from the competition and show why you're the best choice.

Having hired several people over the years, I'll share what I've looked for as both positives and negatives. This certainly won't be a complete picture from the interviewers' side because other people look for other things and have a different decision-making process. Hopefully, the three stories will help to illustrate this point. Realize that decision-making can be impacted sometimes by an unconscious bias to be discussed later in this book. A word of warning, though, you don't want to work for someone who has bias tendencies!

Let's now go back to the five points listed and get into more detail from the perspective of my experience from the interviewer side of the desk:

1. Knowing your SOAR stories that will relate to the requirements of the new job:

Quite often, people just like me don't have the same experience called for in the job posting. However, as the candidate will gain experience over time, I'm looking more for the required skill. I'll ask a question hoping to hear a SOAR story that proves to me that the interviewee has demonstrated the specific skill. During the conversation, I'll ask more probing questions. What I'm looking for at this next level of questions is how the person thinks. How did they think through the planning phase? How did they problem-solve the situation? Did they have cases of working with demanding clients or co-workers, and how did they manage things? If they came up with a new idea, what was the thinking process that got them there? Have they leveraged a solution in another project or role to solve a different but somewhat similar problem?

I was looking for people who could be innovative, problem-solvers and independently manage things on their own. If their stories showed me these abilities, I wasn't too concerned with their actual job experience.

2. Researching the company to understand their business:

I remember interviewing a young man one time. After the obligatory "Nice to meet you," introductions, the first question I asked was, "What do you know about this company?" He gave me a short and halting response. Here we were, not even one minute into the interview, and I already decided not to hire him. Why? It's bad enough not researching the company you want to work for, but my company was a market research firm. We're a research firm, and you didn't bother to spend any time researching us! That was the shortest interview I ever did. I did ask more questions so that he wouldn't be embarrassed, but I didn't want to waste much of his time or mine.

I don't expect the interviewee to know about the company in-depth or even understand much. I'm trying to determine whether they are interested in the company or just interested solely in getting a job. The amount of information they share on this question gives me an idea of how much effort they put into considering applying.

Besides that, it's a good thing for you to find out what is going on at the company lately to see whether this is a place where you want to work.

3. Being prepared with a few key questions:

For me, just like researching the company, if the interviewee had no questions for me, they weren't getting hired. Again, this showed me that they weren't putting any real thought or effort into the process; they just wanted to get a job. These people are not go-getters; they won't drive anything and won't raise team performance.

One perspective for asking questions is demonstrating that you have put time and effort into thinking more deeply about the role. It shows that there are things of importance to you other than just getting the job. It can also demonstrate your level of thinking. I do get impressed when someone asks very thoughtful questions, and you wouldn't expect an outsider to think to that level. Do you want someone on the team that sits in meetings and never asks questions or someone who asks thoughtful questions? For me, you could gain or lose points with your questions.

Another reason for questions is because I believe that the interview process is a two-way street. On the one side of the table, the interviewer wants to make sure that you're right for the job. Equally, on the other side of the table, you want to ensure that the job, company, and potential new manager are the right fit for you. It may be an ideal job, but if the manager is lousy and there's a miserable corporate culture, you're better to pass it up and look for the position in another place. Or maybe the company is excellent, as is the potential new manager, but the role won't be the right fit for you.

To illustrate this latter point, I'll share a story where I was the interviewer. I was hiring for a role with a client-facing element, although most of the time would be spent on operational type tasks. I was doing a phone interview with a young man that, on paper, had related qualifications. The interview started well, and his answers were concrete. His questions, though, made me think there was a misalignment. I began to probe with a different line of questions. It soon became apparent that he was not clear on the actual job requirements. That's okay, as it does happen, and sometimes it's tricky to read a job posting and genuinely understand the responsibilities.

After ten minutes, I stopped the interview by saying, "I don't think this is the kind of job you're wanting." I then identified the misalignment between what he was looking for and what the job entailed. He agreed with the assessment. I did, though, say that he should apply for a client service role at the company. That job would be very aligned with what he wanted to do. I suggested he go back to HR and see if there were any openings for that role. I also offered to inform HR that they should get him interviews in that area if possible.

He appreciated my honesty and offer of support. As I said to him, I don't want to hire anyone where the role will not be something the person would be passionate about even if they could do the work. It wouldn't be fair to them as they'd probably be looking shortly to move on again.

4. Being enthusiastic during the interview:

You would think that this point is a no-brainer, but it isn't for some people. As an interviewer, you know that every interviewee has some anxiety, and that's okay. I watch for this, though, and feel more confident with people who do not appear overly anxious. The best way to combat this is to prepare well for the interview. Being optimally prepared helps your confidence, which reduces anxiety.

Another critical factor I assess is, "Will you be a great fit with the other people on the team?" I'm a firm believer that having the ability to be a great team player and fit well with others is just as vital as having the skills to do the job. When you have the right chemistry across your team, you can make magic happen! People are willing to pitch in and help each other. With positive chemistry, people are more productive and creative. Nobody wants to work with someone who is depressed or a loner, or a constant complainer. Not being a fit hurts chemistry, then productivity and creativity suffer. Part of being a fit always seemed to be a level of enthusiasm. And if you can't be enthusiastic during a critical interview where your best foot needs to be put forward, you'll never be energetic on the job.

5. Sending a post-interview "thank you":

Sending a thank you is just a form of common courtesy. However, I mention it because many people don't do it. In my experience, less than half of the people I interviewed sent a thank you for my time and consideration. I hear lots of people complaining about HR "ghosting" them, but not saying thank you is like "ghosting" the interviewer.

If you don't show this courtesy after an interview, why should you be hired? It almost says you won't be courteous to your co-workers or your clients. What manager would want someone like that on the team? A little tip here. The thank you should be sent within 24 hours at the latest. The reason being, you may have been the last person to be interviewed, and a decision is forthcoming in the next day or two.

Now that we've looked at each high-level item (resume, cover letter, interview), let me share three stories where I was the interviewee. I'm doing this to illustrate that there are factors, other than the posted list of qualifications, that can come into play in the hiring decision. I trust it will help you think of the interview in a different and broader sense. Knowing this can be another type of differentiator where your interview competition focuses just on their job experiences.

This initial story is from my very first job interview after college. At the time, I was quite desperate, financially, to get a job. The role was in Data Collection (DC), and the interview process also involved a timed math test. A week later, I got the job offer! After some months, I was curious and asked my boss why he hired me. As a youth, I had worked at my father's grocery store and gas station in a rural area. I also did other jobs like working on a racehorse farm where tasks included cleaning the stalls, bringing in hay, and washing the horses. This information let my boss know that I would work hard and do the "dirty" jobs. Yes, I had done great on the math test, but he hired me based on his perception of my work ethic. This example shows that you never know what factors will influence the hiring decision, like cleaning out horsesh*t did for me. Yes, I know there's a joke in there somewhere.

The second story is about a job opening in another department that was very intriguing to me. For the first time in my career, it would be an opportunity to work directly with clients. It was also in an IT-type role that I had not handled before. Already, then, you can see that I'm going after a job where I have zero experience to share in these areas and you're right! In going for a position where you have a similar experience, you still must show the interviewer how your experience and skills align well with the job. In this case, I had to do the same thing, but show how different backgrounds and unique skills could transfer to this job.

Knowing that my competition would more than likely have the related experience I lacked, this fact had to get into the conversation. Before the interview, I had thought through how to address this issue. I also thought it best to proactively address so the interviewer could see I had considered what might be regarded as a negative in my application. At what felt like the right moment, I declared, "To be honest, not only I have not used the proprietary software, but I also haven't even seen it. However, it is just software. Excel and PowerPoint are software and I taught myself how to use them so I can quickly learn how to use yours. An important point to consider is that I have the ability for lateral thinking. There will be other interviewees that know how to use the software today, but don't have lateral thinking. They are ahead of me now, but once I learn the software, I'll jump way ahead of them." So, here I was with about 80% of the job involving the software's use, and I'm declaring I've never used it! Instead of hearing "Thanks for applying," the interview carried on.

I was up against seven other interviewees and got the job! A few weeks after starting, I asked my new boss what made him decide to hire me. My declaration of not knowing the software but having lateral thinking ability weighed in on the decision. More importantly, though, was that earlier in my career, I worked in the DC department. One of my peers in this new department had also come from there. One thing my boss noticed about her was a great work ethic. He found out this was not solely because of her character but also because of the discipline required to work in DC. Each month you would get a schedule from your manager identifying what work to complete and the location. You could go the whole month without seeing or speaking to your manager. Some days you would be in a store with other colleagues; you would be working alone on others. You had to be self-disciplined to manage your time to hit multiple deadlines throughout the month and the critical end-of-month deadline.

In the next few years, I proved to my boss that he had made the right choice. We had quarterly all-team meetings, which included the group responsible for designing and building the proprietary software. My ability for lateral thinking allowed me to create reporting techniques that blew the developers away. Once, after I presented a new report at a quarterly meeting, a senior developer told me, "Wow, I never thought anyone would use the software in that way!" Other peers of mine also did some great work, and at times the development team took what we did and coded it into the software so that any user could easily do the same things.

In applying for this role, I took a gamble as I had zero experience with the main job requirement. However, longer-term, it turned out to be the most rewarding gamble of my career. I moved up from this junior developer position to eventually be a Team Leader. Some eight years later, I was selected for an ex-pat assignment where the company moved the family and all our household belongings to Oxford, England, for three years.

I got my first job in Data Collection based on a perceived work ethic from my youth. Twenty years later, I got a job in an IT-type department based on my Data Collection days perceived work ethic! Sometimes you'll see an indication in a job posting around work ethic or habits. Ensure you portray yours during the interview as it may be the difference-maker in a decision!

This last story is from an interview, late in my career, for a leadership role in another department. You're always going to get tricky or challenging questions asked, and sometimes it can put you off balance a bit. While I had substantial and related experiences, the interviewer had one red flag on me. She got the question out relatively early, probably to cut the interview short if she didn't like the answer. She questioned, "Your resume shows you moving between leadership roles and individual contribution roles, why is that?" It was a great and fair question and, fortunately, didn't throw me off. My response was that, at times, I had organically developed into a leadership role. Then I found an individual contributor role that was very intriguing and moved there. Afterwards, I organically grew into a leadership role again. I was comfortable and happy to lead people, but it wasn't a priority for me to always be a leader. I was more interested in the challenge of the role.

The answer eliminated the red flag for her as a few weeks later, she hired me. This story connects to the second interview story, as well. How? I moved to that junior developer role as an individual contributor from leading a small department. This move is what the hiring manager noticed and wondered why I would do such a thing. As noted earlier, going to this junior, individual contributor role turned out to be my career's best move.

You've assessed your skills by using the Skill Set Matrix and getting external feedback. Then went about getting training or experience to improve weak areas by using SMART goals for your development plan. Then tweaked your master resume to get past the ATS system and wrote a great cover letter that got you invited for an interview. During that interview, you shared numerous SOAR stories that helped get you hired. Congratulations, the difficult but short-term part is over! However, now starts the marathon. Fortunately, you can read on to learn the tools to help you drive a successful career.

CHAPTER 4

LEVEL 1 THINKING

This chapter will look at different ways of "thinking" that can significantly help you at work and at home. Some of you may already use all these methods but perhaps will still see something here to expand your understanding. Some of you may use a few of these methods, and others may have never heard of any of them. What this means is that the latter two groups are adding knowledge and skills. Then, perhaps where you have struggled with some things in the past, understanding how these methods work will now enable you to move past similar struggles in the future.

This chapter is challenging as many of these methods will not be an automatic process within your current way of thinking. For those of us with the ability for lateral thinking, some approaches come easily and naturally. For people where it's unnatural, they can develop other ways to think like this. So, like many concepts in this book, the intent here is to raise your awareness and provide tips or ideas to help you leverage additional tools and skills.

Think in A New Box

I truly enjoyed reading, and highly recommend, "Thinking In New Boxes" by Luc de Brabandere and Alan Iny. It's about business creativity with plenty of examples from actual companies. The book highlights how some people and companies think they are innovative, but they are just creating something different within the same box. What they need to do to be truly innovative is to think in terms of a new box. An excellent example is the BIC Company who, in its' early stages, made disposable pens that millions of people used. When BIC looked to innovate their product line, the typical suggestion was a "new colour.". Some thought this was innovative, but that's not real innovation. They were still thinking in the same box. Where new creation began is when they decided to think of the company in different terms. They now decided to think of themselves as a "manufacturer of disposable plastic products." Thinking into this new box by changing the definition of who they were, they added product lines like disposable plastic lighters and disposable plastic razors. Now they were innovative!

From a business growth perspective, merely adding new colours to their pens would possibly cannibalize existing sales. Cannibalization results from someone who used to buy a blue pen now purchasing the new purple pen instead. Stealing sales from yourself doesn't create the desired growth from new products. In this case, sales stay flat instead of growing. By adding lighters and razors to their product line, these sales were incremental and didn't occur at the expense of reduced pen sales. What gets cannibalized here is their competitor sales, which is fantastic!

This thinking needs to be the road for your future success. If what you've been doing to date is not working, you need to think in a new box. Don't try this alone, though, because you're looking through the same lens you've always used. Talk to people whom you value and trust and get them to help with new perspectives. Don't just think of a new colour for your pen!

Right-to-Left Thinking

Most people will have never heard this term before. However, some of them may have used this technique without even realizing it. I've included it again to raise awareness as it's a valuable tool to utilize consciously. Congratulations, if you have already heard of it and use it!

Right-to-left thinking (RTLT) is useful for things like project planning or mapping out a process. In simple terms, RTLT is beginning where you need to finish (the right) and then move step by step to the left, ending where you need to start. In terms of project planning, this may help identify that the work should have started last week!

There are many different types of 'finishes' on the right for using right-to-left. Let's look at an example of building a suite of category management reports to be used by your client. This example is from my Nielsen days. You could use RTLT for both the reports' design and delivery, with the design review occurring first. This order will be a crucial element of project planning for the delivery, seeing as it impacts the three interacting aspects of scope, time, and resource.

Once you have a fix on these items, you can use RTLT for the delivery's project planning. Note: Even though almost none of you will build reports in your career, this example should help you visualize how the process can work for you.

Design: If you want to go to the extreme right, you will say the ultimate goal is to maximize profitability to keep shareholders happy and secure the company's financial health. Yes, that could be the extreme right for many things at the company. Moving to the left, it's about beating the competition, having the products that consumers love and having the right pricing and promotions. To do this, you need to have critical insights to determine the best course of action. This now requires us to set up multiple RTLT branches to feed the ultimate endpoint on the right. I say multiple because the decisions made further to the left will differ based on each reports' critical insights. In a way, you can take a hierarchy of reports, tip it 90 degrees to the right, and use RTLT there as well.

After you've decided on the mix of reports, the next decision is on the insights required for action. What are the questions to be asked, and what data provides the answers? This information helps you move further to the left to decide how you get to those insights quickly through analysis. There are multiple design questions here, such as:

- Whether you need to colour code data based on parameters?
- Does sorting the data in specific ways help get actionable items to the top of page 1?
- Are there lines you can hide, or maybe even not retrieve because they are only 'excessive data noise' on the report?
- What are the key facts you need from the data or are there key facts that you need to create from the available data, such as a benchmark calculation?

Now you know the insights required for a report to answer the clients' questions. The next step is to define the most efficient set of data to retrieve from the entire database. This exercise allows reports to be run faster and contain less 'excessive data noise,' which benefits the client. (What I'm terming 'excessive data noise' is data a user is forced to look at but wouldn't assist in decision-making.) You could now determine the best selection of products, markets, time frames and facts required for decisions. Is knowing the insights and analysis needed plus optimal data set all there is to it? No. There is one more step in the process to support speed to insights. That is the layout of the data, which almost no one ever thinks about. Let me share an example to illustrate what this means.

Our Retail Services (RS) associate brought me the specifications for a single report build from their meeting with their retailer contact. I looked at the requirements and asked how the client wanted the data laid out. The answer was, "Whatever way you think." I responded that it shouldn't be based on what I thought, but rather on what insights the retailer was looking to get. He would be in a much better position to know what he was looking for. With our proprietary software, you could have dimensions (product, market, time frame, facts) in the rows and the columns at a minimum and in the 'pages.' We could also put multiple dimensions in any of these locations. For example, you could have products in the rows, then markets and facts in the columns with markets nested underneath the facts and then the periods in the pages. Or the periods could be in the columns and markets in the pages. In all, there were about 24 ways that you could lay out the same set of data. Whichever layout gives the quickest speed to the insights should be the decision-maker.

I asked to meet with the retailer to go through this exercise, which the RS associate readily agreed to. Sitting in the retailers' office, I explained the different ways, then started swapping the data into the various layouts. "Can you see your insights easily here?" "No." Swap the data around. "How about now? Can you see your insights easily?" "No." Swap the data around. On the 8th time I swapped the data, the retailer said, "That's it!" He had a question that the report needed to answer, and he could get to it quickly in this 8th layout version. He appreciated our consideration in this area. He knew this was time well spent because it would save him more time than that down the road.

Delivery: RTLT can be the basis of project planning (discussed more in the next chapter), where you start with the date by which you need to deliver the reports and work backwards. Occasionally, I had to use this process when the sales team had committed a delivery timing to the client without checking with me first. I'd use RTLT starting with the committed delivery date and work to the left to see if it were feasible. Sometimes it was, then sometimes I needed to adjust other plans to make it work. On a few occasions, I had to get sales to go back to the client with a realistic delivery date. As a bonus, this process confirmed if we could deliver as requested and simultaneously allowed for creating the project plan.

There may also be multiple sections and layers of RTLT required for large projects. Let's look at an example where your client will be launching new products. Starting from the far right and moving to the left, you plot out that:

- The client wants the in-store launch to occur thirty weeks from now.
- They need to have retailer meetings eight weeks beforehand to get the approval to add their items to the shelves. This date is a hard date to allow the retailer to take the necessary steps internally.

- With twenty-two weeks left, how much time will the client need to analyze your data and prepare presentations? Let's say this is six weeks.
- You also find out that some client analysts need training on your software tool and the reports. This requirement creates another question, which is "How long before the training date will your trainers need with the final solution to properly prepare their lesson package?" Let's say they need two weeks.
- As well, some of these analysts will also need the software installed. The due date here is the day before training. The good news here is that we can work on these steps concurrently rather than consecutively.
- We now have fourteen weeks remaining using RTLT. You'll want the key contact to conduct some UAT and sign off on all the reports before you hand them to training. Hopefully, you can acquire sign-off on individual reports as you go along to take the pressure off this deadline. If you can't, though, you need to put in extra time for some back and forth with the client. Let's say that three weeks are required.
- We're now down to eleven weeks, by which we must build all reports. As you previously estimated the building work to be eight weeks, the client needs to sign the proposal three weeks from now. If they sign by that date, off goes your report builder. If they don't sign by then, it means having to either reduce scope or increase resources to hit those other dates that are immovable. At least you now know there is a favourable project plan with dates that can work for all involved.

I used RTLT in terms of project planning for this book. On the far right, I wanted it to be available for the Christmas gift-giving season. Therefore, a release deadline of Friday, November 27, 2020, was set. In Chapter 5, you'll see the details of the resulting project plan that helped steer me.

Lean Six Sigma

You may be looking at the title and thinking, "I can skip this section because I'll never work in the manufacturing field for which Lean Six Sigma was developed." I trust that the stories included in this section will show why you shouldn't skip ahead. I wasn't manufacturing consumer products, but you'll see how the Six Sigma tool improved quality and delivery timing in an existing process; and created a new data product.

But first, let's start with a delightful story of how Six Sigma helped one of my colleagues in her home life. Our department had "communities," which were groups of employees focusing on bringing improvements or innovation to existing tasks. Some of the topics were category standards design, working with third parties, and User Acceptance Testing (UAT). One of my direct reports, Leah, was a Six Sigma Black Belt and suggested that we should start a BPI (Business Process Improvement) community. I would be the sponsor and work with her on vision and objectives. She would create and deliver the content. We felt that sharing Lean Six Sigma concepts and practices could be utilized by our colleagues to help make their jobs more efficient, thereby improving their job satisfaction. The great thing about Lean Six Sigma is that it creates a structure to follow. This framework, if followed correctly, will lead to fixing problems and driving improvements.

We set up bi-weekly calls to get things rolling and were joined by a relatively large group in the initial meetings. I think the fact that we could help them eliminate waste, save time, and ease pressure was quite attractive to them. Also keeping people engaged was Leah's leadership on the calls and creating interactive content. She is a firm believer that "The best way to learn is by having fun learning." People certainly don't want to only listen for an hour every time. On one of the calls, she taught a tool that would help make decisions on organizing things. It can certainly be used outside of the manufacturing process and was her favourite – the Lean Spaghetti diagram. The tools' purpose is to eliminate unnecessary actions and make things more efficient. Who doesn't want to do that? You draw connections from one step to another from beginning to end, which creates a picture of the process. When completed, the look of your diagram will reveal if you have an efficient process (only a few lines here and there) or an inefficient process (multiple lines crossing themselves several times and looking like a pile of spaghetti on the page!).

To end the call, Leah challenged everyone to pick a task upon which to apply the tool. In the next meeting, she asked people to share what they did and the results they got. To us, the most intriguing feedback was from a colleague in the US. She felt that her kitchen and pantry were always disorganized, so this was her situation for applying the tool. She proudly reported that Lean had helped her get the kitchen reorganized in the most efficient manner in her life! This outcome was a fabulous example of how you can learn things that are a transferrable skill to other jobs or your personal life.

To see what the tool would show you, here's something you can map out in your own home. This exercise will show how efficient your kitchen is set-up to make a cup of coffee or tea. Start by drawing your kitchen layout and mark where you have the cups, saucers, coffee, sugar, cream/milk, spoons, kettle, or coffeemaker, sink and anything else that's relative. Then, draw a line from entering the kitchen to each of these items in the order you usually follow.

Win It, Drive It!

This process will create your spaghetti diagram of how you move around the kitchen to make a simple cup of coffee/tea.

Do you walk past the fridge and cutlery drawer to first get a cup? Then walk back to get a spoon, then back again to get the kettle, then to the sink, which is past where the coffee is stored, then past the coffee one more time to plug in the kettle, then past the cutlery drawer for a third time to get the milk...? Map this out and see if you have just a few efficient lines or a massive plate of spaghetti. Now for some fun. If there are a few of you in the house that make coffee; each should draw their diagram. Whoever has the least amount of spaghetti is the most efficient and wins!

Does it make sense now why you should read about this topic even if you aren't going to work in a manufacturing company? By the way, while most communities eventually folded, this one is still active some four years later! Also, while all the others were internal department only, we gladly extended BPI membership to Nielsen colleagues outside our department. They were hearing that people were learning this valuable information and were having fun in the process. So, they wanted in. We gladly agreed to expand membership due to the value of the learnings. This knowledge would help everyone plus be a significant benefit for the business.

Six Sigma is a set of tools and processes for process improvement, designed initially to almost eliminate all manufacturing defects. It's almost, as the goal is 99.99966% defect-free, meaning that .00034% defects are acceptable. In other words, only 1 defect out of 294,118 instances, so not that bad!

The term, Six Sigma, was registered as a Motorola trademark back in 1993. A manufacturing process's maturity can be described by a *sigma* rating indicating its' yield percentage of defect-free products it creates. As the mathematics take into consideration standard deviations of a normal distribution... Sorry, but it's too complicated for me to explain in layman's terms. As you can guess, though, Motorola set a goal of "six" for all its' manufacturing, hence Six Sigma.

You may have also heard the term Lean, a methodology to address process flow and waste issues in manufacturing. Combining Lean with Six Sigma, which focuses on variation and design, you achieve better business and operational excellence through Lean Six Sigma. There are various levels of "belts" within Six Sigma, like martial arts. The first level is White, in which simply understand the concept but don't participate in any BPI project. Next is Yellow, where you would get basic training in the tools then complete a project. This belt is the one we hoped to get for people involved in our community. Unfortunately, new senior leadership at Nielsen shut down the whole BPI organization before proper certifications were in play. Green belts have a deeper understanding than Yellow and will be involved in project implementation under the direction of a Black Belt. This work, the Yellow and Green Belts will do on top of their regular job. However, a Black Belt devotes 100% of their time to Six Sigma projects and is responsible for project execution and leadership of tasks under a Master Black Belt direction. The Master BB works full-time with the Black Belts and Project Champions across multiple projects to ensure consistent application of Six Sigma across all functions and departments.

Like many other topics included here, there are all sorts of books, online courses, and in-house training available on Lean Six Sigma. Also, if you're currently a Premium member on LinkedIn, you have access to LinkedIn Learning. Here you will find lots of videos on Six Sigma, Lean, and Kaizen. There are also videos for White, Yellow,

Green and Black belts. Put aside some time, though, as some belts have 20+ hours of video content!

Something extra is that there's a professional body that manages the issuance of formal certificates for achieving the various belts. Some readers will need to get these certifications based on the roles they will have. If not today, then perhaps in the future, depending on how high they want to get in specific areas of a company. As with the Skill Set Matrix exercise, look at your future career path. Are any of those potential roles expecting or preferring you to have a Six Sigma belt? If yes, then Lean Six Sigma will be a certification requirement rather than a 'nice to know.' Other readers won't need the certification as it's not a requirement for their jobs. However, a certificate could be a 'differentiator' versus many of your competitors in winning interviews or achieving promotions.

At this point, you may feel that the above scenarios do not apply to you, but there is still great value in this knowledge. You're correct! Even without getting a certificate, a general understanding of the concepts and tools will help at one or more points in your life. You will be able to use this information <u>to your advantage</u> throughout your career or even at home, as illustrated earlier. To highlight how that can happen, let me now share stories from my various roles. I trust that they will reveal a variety of circumstances and ways for using this knowledge. FYI, for these examples, I was only involved as a subject matter expert; I didn't have a belt. Nor had I undertaken any training sessions.

I had just started in a sales and service role, and one of my clients was complaining about their global database almost always delivered late. This situation was such a sore point that they were going to start asking for refunds to compensate. Naturally, you don't want to be giving money back. On top of that, our company was trying to upsell them to a new global solution. More concerning, then, was the risk to an upcoming sale if deliveries continued this lateness pattern. My new boss couldn't give me any background for the on-going cause but wanted it fixed a.s.a.p. So, I started by employing a thought process that was logical to me. I didn't realize it at the time, but it turns out that I was using the Six Sigma DMAIC process, which stands for Define, Measure, Analyze, Improve, and Control.

For the Define step, I had calls with the offshore team leader responsible for creating the database each month. I found out which input databases they were getting from where, and their process from receipt of input database to the final client database release.

For the Measure step, I asked for data covering the last three months. This information included the expected and actual receipt date and load date for every internal database. Some input databases had one expected delivery date and two delivery dates. A dual delivery would happen if the third party found errors and asked the local country to fix and re-run the database. Or if the local country found issues, re-ran then re-delivered the database. I also contacted each country to compare its database creation date versus the date by which the third party received the database. A final, key measure was the expected and actual delivery date to the client.

In the Analyze step, I noticed that many databases were not loaded up to a full week after receipt by the third party. If they found errors, the re-run database took another week or more to be delivered, compounding the problem. Also apparent was that many databases were received very close to the client committed deadline. Therefore, any errors in them made it extremely difficult to turnaround a re-run database in time. I also noticed some lags between expected and actual dates from local. Some lags were due to the country focusing on local client deliveries and doing the global delivery later in the schedule. When I asked the third party if they knew why there were a few large lags, the answer was that sometimes the countries forgot to send the database or thought they did when they didn't.

An issue that seemed easy to remedy was the lags of the local Nielsen countries and the third party. A local lag was particularly harmful when their database's local delivery date was close to the global client deadline. The third-party lag was due to them holding received databases until they received enough to keep someone busy for a full day. This lag hurt most when they sat on a database with errors that would need to be re-run and re-delivered. As mentioned, some of the databases they sat on for a full week! The conclusion, then, was that we just needed to move to a "when ready" process. Plus, both sides needed to be more proactive in working together and managing a tight data flow.

For the Improve step, I asked local Nielsen to deliver the database to the third party on the day it was released locally. Don't wait, and don't forget! Next, if there was an issue locally creating a delay, then a new date needed to be immediately updated with the third party to avoid follow-up on their part. Most importantly, if the third party informed them of an error, they needed to recreate the database as a priority. This step would be beneficial for their local client as well.

Then, for the third party, if a database didn't arrive by the date expected, I asked them to contact local Nielsen the next day and not just sit there and wait. In this way, if locals made a simple mistake of forgetting (and it happens), they could ship the database right then and there. Secondly, I asked them to start loading every input database within 24 hours of receipt. Yes, this would mean multiple loads during the week instead of just one or two. However, this was clearly an issue, mainly if they found errors. Finally, I asked them to let me know if they had any problems or delays with local Nielsen, and I would step in to help expedite things if possible.

For the final step of Control, I asked the third party to provide me with the scheduling report that they used. I also wanted the updated information sent to me daily. I got to see the dates for expected delivery from local, actual delivery, load, re-runs, re-delivery, the client's expected and exact delivery dates. I could then "ride shotgun" and query the third party if dates didn't fit our new "when ready" timing. I did this for three months, and from the first time we implemented the new process onward, the global client delivery was always on time.

It's not rocket science, but this is an excellent example of how looking at things by following the Six Sigma structure can significantly help. It should also illustrate that you can leverage this tool without being an expert or taking extensive training. It's about using the structure along with some logic and a 'flexible curiosity mindset.'

This second story was another major project, in progress for several months, with a large, global client and their third-party support based in India. We provided data extractions from hundreds of local databases to the third party, who then mapped our data to the clients' definition. They sent those files to the client, who then loaded them into their internal data warehouse. To this point, we had delivered all the work as per the agreements. However, the third party now started to complain each week to the client and always blaming us. This tongue-wagging made the client begin to think that the process was taking too much time.

It always creates a problematic situation when you continuously have a competitor in the client's ear, feeding them volumes of incorrect information. Why do I call the third party a competitor? We could, and did propose, to do the same mapping work like them. However, the client got convinced that the third party could do the job at a much lower cost.

I could write an entire chapter about a meeting I attended at the client's mid-town Manhattan office that included the third-party project manager. Suffice it to say, I ably explained and disproved all the "problems" highlighted by the PM. My commentary quieted things down to a degree with the client. It also resulted in us agreeing that we needed a review meeting to discuss several items. I offered to get a Nielsen Black Belt to lead a BPI session. As the projects' participants were spread from North America to India, the meetings' logical mid-point was at the Nielsen office in Oxford, England. A bonus for me was the opportunity to go back to the location of my ex-pat assignment. It would be like going back to my second home for a week.

In advance of the meetings, the Black Belt had several conversations with all the participants. He was looking to define the problem and prepare which tools we would use and in what order. It also allowed him to get up to speed quickly on the situation from everyone's perspective. His analysis of the case determined that we would need to spend 2.5-3 days to work through everything, and he was right. He then crafted an agenda so everyone would know that this would be a very intensive exercise.

I was able to book a massive room that we could keep for the full three days. Having the same room was valuable as a Six Sigma event can have you taping an awful lot of paper or putting up post-it notes and string all over the walls. And you don't want to be pulling it all down at night and putting it back up in another room the next day! Taping things to the wall was in full force in our case. We went through the '5 Whys', put up fishbone diagrams, control charts, business process maps and Pareto charts. These were on top of the value stream mapping and SIPOC (Suppliers, Inputs, Process, Outputs, Customers) analysis the Black Belt had pulled together before the meeting. Then, another wall that started with blank flipcharts became populated over time with all our future action items.

What I loved most about this process was that it was a very safe way to show the client that, in specific ways, *they were part of the problem*. The biggest problem here was that the client was a bottleneck in the process. Everything from us to the third party had to flow through only two people at the client. Everything from the third party to the clients' internal team had to flow through the same two people! This bottleneck meant that our deliveries just sat there and didn't move forward when they worked on third party deliveries.

Finally, and most importantly for us, the Six Sigma process forced everyone to be objective and didn't allow you to hide or bullsh*t everyone. The process revealed the truth behind a lot of the third-parties' complaints and accusations. The client was now getting a different picture of reality versus the one painted in New York. Of course, the skill of the Black Belt in unearthing the truth was of extreme value.

At the end of this 3-day session, we had 72 action items to address everything uncovered. This outcome highlighted why things were not progressing as hoped and the extreme value of the cost and time to run this session. Although there were some hard costs to attend the meeting, there were cost savings down the road as people stopped doing checks identified as redundant. The Oxford session occurred in February, and we met again in May at the clients' office in New York for a closing follow-up. We were delighted when the Black Belt announced that he'd never seen such a commitment before. Of the 72 action items from February, 70 were closed, with the final two planned for completion shortly. We were also able to confirm the improvement in workflow, time savings, quality improvements and reduction of third-party complaints. All around, a fantastic success!

This third story involves the same client. In this case, the request was to supply data from a different product but in a similar way. Therefore, determining what to send, quality check parameters, reporting needs, and other requirements were all very different. Instead of repeating history, we decided to use another Six Sigma process to get the project started in a much better way. The tool used here was <u>DMADV</u>, which stands for Define, Measure, Analyze, Design, and Verify.

The challenge in rolling this project out was even more significant than the previous one. For starters, we would again be dealing with the same third party. On top of that, the client was buying the same data type in many countries from one of our major global competitors. The same meetings, then, would also include this competitor, which made for fascinating conversations. In hindsight, I will admit that the competitors' representatives were very cooperative and professional in their approach. This behaviour certainly helped to create productive meetings. The same Nielsen Black Belt was involved, and as you would expect, he managed things from a professional, unbiased position. In many ways, Six Sigma doesn't allow for bias as it gets to the truth of the matter.

Perhaps it was also the character of the individuals involved, but Six Sigma's structure helped us work side by side towards the common end goal as if we were all on the same team. The meetings allowed us to define what was needed, how it must be delivered, any supporting material, the responsible party for each step, and a timeline for the project. Like our Oxford meeting, it was multiple days but worth every minute and dollar. Here, the tricky part is that you can't calculate the savings versus not having these meetings by starting the project with these designed efficiencies. However, after having done about five of these events, I knew there would be significant savings in time and money.

Here's one final story to highlight more value with the Six Sigma process. I was working in our Oxford, UK office, and my role changed from leading a team building reports for clients in the UK and Ireland to clients across Europe. Based on the scope change impact, I wanted an end-to-end review using <u>DMADV</u> to make sure we got things up and running correctly.

The workshop lasted a full two days. There were a dozen attendees from the various departments that would be involved. As a group, we started identifying each step beginning with the client's request. We wrote each action or decision or document on different colours and shapes of Post-It notes. Then the notes were taped onto the wall, with coloured strings connecting them in a step-by-step manner. We were actively creating a giant flowchart! At times, the chart building stopped as we needed to debate who should be responsible for specific tasks or how long things should take. While people were cooperative, they were also looking to protect their turf and resources.

The Black Belt (a different one) did a great job asking probing questions when the group got stuck or were at odds. By the end of the second day, there were notes and strings stretching the entire 24-foot (7.3 meters) width of the wall and about 50% of the vertical space. It was quite the picture to behold, so we all took a few as a remembrance. As you can imagine, one of the great things coming out of this workshop is that we had defined the entire end-to-end process with decision points and actions plus confirmed what documentation was required to support being successful. This outcome is what you would expect. The added value, though, was that there were four steps in the process identified as necessary, and no one claimed it should be their responsibility. No one could even say, exactly, who should be responsible. This discovery created a critical action point, coming out of the meetings, to conclude who should be accountable. We couldn't move end-to-end without someone managing these steps. That would be like building a car, with no one on the production line was identified as responsible for installing the wheels!

I firmly believe there is great value in having a full-time, dedicated BPI organization for massive corporations. I saw so many ways to improve quality, delivery, reduced working hours, improved customer satisfaction, proved third party complaints to be invalid, and built better processes right upfront to know it's worth the cost. Typically, you are required to calculate a cost/benefit on each project to confirm this assumption before you even approve of moving ahead. So, if you know this work is paying for itself while generating other benefits, why wouldn't you do it?

Along with this, though, the BPI organization should also create communities like we did to share the knowledge. They can get people to have a 'flexible curiosity mindset' and drive continuous improvement. If a corporation doesn't want a dedicated organization's expense, it will help to, at least, proactively recruit individuals with a Six Sigma certification. They are trained in the process and could create such communities.

A small and medium-sized business would not have a BPI organization but should similarly hire people who certification. I'm positive that most companies will have one or more essential elements that could be improved using Lean Six Sigma. If I'm wrong, then hats off to you for having a remarkably well-run business!

From an individual perspective, it is a differentiator if you have a Six Sigma Black Belt certificate, no matter the job. Whatever you needed to do to achieve the certification should be one of your SOAR stories during an interview. Even if you don't want to get a belt, understanding the concept at a high level, applying that knowledge, and achieving success can be a SOAR story. Mine was. I would certainly take notice if an interviewee told me that, although they didn't have a Six Sigma black belt, this is how they used the DMAIC or DMADV process for success in their last job. That's what I'm looking for, not just someone able to do a job, but the extra knowledge or in-depth thought process they go through to innovate, solve problems, or create efficiencies. These are the things that make a difference in you and in hiring or promotion decisions.

However, if thinking in Six Sigma terms does not seem to be something you can do, here's a question. Can you develop a "change management" mindset? What do I mean by that? Let me share what one of my direct reports said was the main thing she learned from me. She noticed that the department kept pushing projects and clients to me that were in terrible shape. Also, I didn't automatically let it keep going as before but would immediately and always be asking questions. I was doing so with a "change management" mindset.

What did I do? Firstly, I asked the people how the service worked, problems encountered, and the history of how and why they did things the current way. Usually, these people knew the process was messy and had issues but kept doing it as had always been done. Additionally, some staff were so busy that they didn't have the time to see if they could improve the process. Ironically, as you can guess, they were overloaded because the process was messy and overly time-consuming. So, with the mindset elements of "Kaizen" and "Stay Curious," I would always start to look at how to improve the current way of doing things. As you would expect, the older the solution, the more opportunity there was for improvement. Why? There were numerous reasons, such as:

- Helpful tools were now around that didn't exist when they first built the solution
- People were doing things manually, and someone on my team knew how to create an Excel macro to automate specific steps
- I could help them apply learnings from other projects
- Sometimes we delivered things the client didn't use anymore, but no one on their side said to stop, and no one on our side asked
- People were doing it that way because they were told to
- People didn't have the time to analyze and investigate whether they could improve the process
- People didn't have the skill or experience to analyze the situation
- There was a third party involved in the process, and they got paid whether things were efficient or not
- You had a problem like in Hans Christian Andersen's story "The Emperor's New Clothes" where, in this context, no one wanted to tell the boss that things weren't working well
- …

In conclusion, there are three levels in terms of this Six Sigma section. The first level is to achieve Six Sigma belts progressively. The second is, like me, to not have an actual belt but be able to use the structure to solve problems and create efficiencies. The final level is, at a minimum, to have a "change management" mindset. Don't think that you always need to keep doing it the way it has always been done! Having one of these levels will help throughout your entire career, no matter where you go.

Thought Leadership

Some people detest or are bored with the term "thought leadership." You may be one of them. However, for our purposes here, you don't have to use that term, but rather think and operate within the definition. You don't have to put this label on what you will do, instead impress, and attract people to you by delivering what it's meant to accomplish.

You could define thought leadership as "pioneering new ideas rather than following conventional wisdom." The Oxford dictionary defines it as "intellectual influence and innovative or pioneering thinking." Your ideas must focus on answering the most critical questions that your target audience has today to gain real and instant traction. To deliver against thought leadership means you deeply understand your business, your customers' needs and the marketplace in which you operate. Being a thought leader means you are highly respected and in-demand by clients, peers, co-workers, or outside interests. You and your ideas are much sought-after expertise, so what better place to be!

Companies can position themselves as "thought leaders" as a marketing ploy to attract clients away from their competitors. They are using it to increase revenue and profits. You can openly use thought leadership to help others, thereby marketing yourself. In linking back to the Skill Set Matrix, ratings on Hard Skills and Industry Knowledge need to be Master level to consider yourself capable of being a thought leader in your area. Any gaps shouldn't discourage you but highlight another benefit and end goal for continued self-development.

In addition to being a master of the topic, another critical point is that you must regularly read and research in this area. You must know what else is out there on the subject that improves your knowledge or gives you something upon which to position an educated opinion. This reading and research may spark other new ideas and innovation, which is what thought leadership is all about.

This reminds me of a story I read about Tom Hanks's acceptance speech at the Golden Globes while receiving the Cecil B. DeMille Award for "outstanding contributions to the world of entertainment." Tom recalled the most valuable lesson he learned very early in his career. In his first professional job he, and some fellow interns, showed up at rehearsal after too much partying the night before. They all got reamed out by the director. According to Hanks, the director screamed at them and asked, "You know what your job is? You have got to show up on time, and you must know the text, and you have to have a head full of ideas. Otherwise, I can't do my job." When the director says, "you have to know the text, and you have to have a head full of ideas…" to me, he's asking Tom and the others to be thought leaders. He wants them to know the text to a master level to be innovative, which will produce a better product. This learning went a long way to help Tom Hanks become one of the most popular actors of all time.

You also need to have irrefutable data to build your credibility. This is crucial for people to take you seriously. And to be considered a thought leader, several people need to take you seriously and validate you in this way. I didn't know anyone who tried to publish things to demonstrate personal thought leadership. I sure didn't! Lots of us came up with great ideas but didn't position it as thought leadership, nor continue to stay on top of things like we needed to.

The bottom line is that you will work in a particular field where you can build up a mastery over time. Don't forget to present your ideas and continue to carry on in a "thought leadership" mode. This action will differentiate you from the crowd! Also, while companies typically do this externally for their clients, there's no reason you can't do this internally at your company.

Here's another exercise for you. Consider these questions. Do you have mastery of a topic in your field? Are you as up to date as possible with what's going on in your industry? If you answered yes both times, then what is the most critical question in your area today? Now, are you able to answer that question with an innovative idea and supporting data? If you're not at a master level yet, that's okay. Your exercise will then be to develop yourself to that level to do the exercise above later in your career.

Diversity and Unconscious Bias

While differentiation can apply to both people and things, diversity applies only to people. Diversity includes many different characteristics. It can be things like race, culture, age, sex, or beliefs. Unfortunately, many people instantly get uncomfortable with people who are different from them. They may not want to work with them or maybe even talk to them. Sadly, this is often from making an external judgment of the individual rather than getting to know them as a person first.

Diversity is of great value at work. How many ice cream flavours would a group of ten white males, all in their 30s and the same culture, create? How many ice cream flavours would the second group of ten, where half were female, ages ranged from 20 to 60 and three or four cultures were represented, create? It would be great if people appreciated human beings' diversity like they crave different ice cream flavours. Do you think Baskin-Robbins would have over 8,000 stores in more than 50 countries if they only sold vanilla ice cream? Their stores make available 31 flavours so that you can try a different flavour every day for an entire month. Consider, too, that in the 75+ years the company has been in business, they've created 1300+ flavours!

Please embrace diversity recognizing the added value it can bring. That's part of one key mindset element, which is "stay curious." I genuinely hope you are there already or, if you aren't, then you will eventually get to the next level in this area. At that point, you'll proactively seek people that are diverse to yourself and your way of thinking. This action will help drive terrific success for yourself and those around you. If we can all do it, then the world will become a much better place.

For the most part, we are aware of the biases that we hold. You can define bias as prejudice <u>in favour of or against</u> one person, group or thing compared with another, usually in an unfair manner. We all have multiple biases, some that are unfortunately serious and dangerous. Then others are a little silly. For example, I have a bias against the flavour of black licorice. Why? As a young child, I was at a baseball tournament one weekend. To cut the story short, I ate so much black licorice that day that I threw up over and over and could taste nothing but that licorice flavour. Since then, I won't eat <u>anything</u> with that flavour and haven't even been keen on the smell! In many ways, simple little events like this can create a bias for years to come.

On the dangerous side, biases unfairly hurt people. They impact people everywhere daily. The challenging aspect here is that it's complicated to prove that the decision-making involved discrimination. A good example here is the ageism bias in the hiring process. This bias mainly hurts the older worker. They may have lots of skills, are far more experienced than younger workers and have been through lots of challenging times. However, they get discounted by HR or the hiring manager because "They're old." I read a story where a senior citizen who still wanted to work applied for a job for which he was well qualified. His resume and cover letter got him past the Human Resources manager for an interview. The phone interview went exceptionally well, so he was invited for an in-person meeting for continued conversations. The gentleman was very excited, feeling that the next interview would end in a job offer. However, when he walked into the office, the hiring manager was able to see that he was an older worker. Suddenly, the enthusiasm disappeared, positivity declined, and in short order, the meeting ended with no job offer. Now you can't prove that an ageism bias was in play in the decision, but the hiring manager's distinct and drastic change would indicate that to be the case.

Some men have a conscious bias against hiring women, concerned about them needing several months off when they have children. Some women may not want to have any men on the team. Some bias has the label of racism when you discount someone due to skin colour. Hopefully, neither you nor anyone with whom you work or socialize holds these kinds of conscious biases. I say 'conscious' because the person knows for a fact that they will not hire an older worker or a woman or someone of colour. They make their decisions based on these single elements and nothing else.

All those examples are thought of as a negative bias because they generate decisions "against" someone. There are other kinds of discrimination which people position as being positive. The reason being that the decision tilts "for" someone. An example of this is a hiring manager who only hires people who graduated from his alma mater. This slant is a positive "for" anyone that graduated from his school but a negative "against" all other graduates. In real terms, this bias is damaging to the hiring manager as well as those graduates. That's because the discrimination has diluted the pool of candidates and potentially eliminated the best candidate around. So there truly is no entirely positive bias. They all hurt someone, including you, somehow.

What then is unconscious bias? It's the same definition as above with the added proviso that you are not aware that your decisions or actions are bias based. Let me give you an example from my life. One night I met a man at an event. We exchanged greetings, and instantly one side of my brain was saying, "I don't like this guy at all!" Fortunately, the other side of my brain asked, "How can you not like him, he just said hello?" The other side proclaimed that there was something about how he looked that generated this instant dislike. The smart side dug deeply into my memory bank and found the reason for this dislike. That side declared, "You don't like him because he looks exactly like the adult version of that kid you had a fight with, in grade school!" The unconscious bias side thought, "Oh my goodness, you're right, he does look like that kid!" This realization changed everything immediately because I knew that my unconscious bias was wholly unfair and without merit. As you would imagine, the guy turned out to be quite pleasant.

There are a few challenging aspects of this kind of bias. The first is that you don't actively realize that it's at work in your brain. Secondly, this unfair bias can frequently exist based on ridiculous reasoning. I once read about a male hiring manager who didn't like a candidate although they were well qualified. Upon reflection, he realized that the woman's dress was the same design and colour as his former girlfriend used to wear. Unconsciously, the dress brought back many painful memories, leading the manager to think of the candidate negatively. This unconscious bias drove the invalid and unfair decision not to hire this qualified candidate.

Stereotyping creates a bias that can exist as both conscious and unconscious. And, unfortunately, stereotyping is usually the result of invalid inputs. Examples are how a particular group of people are portrayed on TV, by the media, through tasteless jokes… Without even meeting and interacting with people from that group, individuals can already have a negative bias. Stop for a moment and think of what stereotypes you may be applying against someone from Japan, Ireland, Russia, or Nigeria. How about someone covered in tattoos, people with dreadlocks or having lots of body piercings? Do you immediately have an unfavourable picture in your mind with any of these groups? Does experience validate it, or does it exist just because of what you've read or seen on TV?

I worked in the market research industry for decades. One element that stayed true the entire time was to ensure that the research "sample size" was large enough to create valid enough information for informed decisions and actions. If enough people don't purchase a specific product, we would hide its' data in buying behaviour studies. The reason being you couldn't derive proper conclusions from just a few people. You need to keep this in mind with people, especially if your first encounter is negative. Don't suddenly paint the entire group with that same brush. Find a way to give someone else a chance, so you don't create an invalid bias.

Just as much as we need to eliminate conscious bias from our mindset, we also need to eliminate unconscious bias. The obvious question here is, "How will I know when to eliminate something that happens unconsciously?" If this were a live meeting, I'd have to proclaim the standard, "That's a great question!" Yes, it is challenging to control something done unconsciously. In this case, we need our other senses to kick in and to listen to them. Much like mine did when there was no logical reason for me to dislike that gentleman instantly. Other instances may be why we get that odd sensation in our stomachs. Perhaps this is the unconscious trying to send a message that we are applying bias while unaware. So, in future, watch out for these signals and sense-check some decisions, particularly those that would unfairly go against someone else. Think through whether it's possible that for some hidden reason, you took an instant dislike or you wouldn't hire them although they're qualified.

Like conscious bias, which in its' most vile form is racism, we need to guard against and overcome unconscious bias!

Cultural Differences Human Similarities

Thinking in the term "cultural differences, human similarities" came to me very late in my career. Mainly because in most of my early career, the only real cultural differences I had to deal with were English and French in Canada. While friends and colleagues had parents or grandparents from various European countries, they were born and raised in Canada. There were unique, cultural observances happening in their homes, but they were all typical Canadians outside the home.

However, in the latter part of my career, I worked internationally for several years. I was fortunate to spend three years working out of the Oxford, UK office dealing with people across Europe. After returning home to Canada, I worked with US-based global clients and led a team spread across Europe and the Americas, supported by a third-party company based in India. Across those years, I led or worked with people in the following countries (those in **bold** are where I had people reporting to me): Argentina, Austria, Australia**,** Brazil, **Canada, Chile,** China, Cyprus, Denmark, **England, France**, Finland, **Germany,** Hungary, India, Ireland, **Italy,** Malaysia, **Mexico**, **Netherlands,** New Zealand, **Norway, Poland,** Portugal, **Romania**, Russia, Spain, Sweden, Switzerland, Turkey, Ukraine, **US,** and **Wales***.

* Most people would include England and Wales as "the UK." However, my direct report who lived in Wales made it very clear in our first conversation that he was to be referenced as working from Wales, not England or the UK because he was Welsh, not English. So, all these years later, I'm still honouring that request.

While working out of the Oxford office, I noticed a trend that leads to stereotyping. Whenever we had a conference call, you knew that the German associates would be on time, whereas our Italian colleagues were often late. It's not my intention to reinforce stereotypes or pass judgment, but it just seemed to be a noticeable cultural difference.

I once read a story where a similar multi-country team leader was perplexed about why the attendees from Japan rarely spoke up during the team calls. She decided to dig into this question and got her clear, cultural difference answer. Her Japanese team did not want to speak on any agenda items without first having the time to consider the topics carefully. Unfortunately for them, she was not sending the agenda out until just before the call. This circumstance left them with no time to prepare appropriately. With the new knowledge of this cultural difference, she started to send the agenda a day in advance. This change now gave the Japanese team time to consider the topics, and they began participating in future calls. Thankfully, a simple resolution to a surprise situation based on culture.

For the most part, we assume that because everyone on the team is doing the same job, they should approach things in the same way. We start to paint everyone in the same role with the same brush, forgetting that there could be cultural differences. However, instead of ignoring differences, there is a team-building opportunity if you recognize and celebrate them! One of the things we did on an early team call was to get everyone to present their answers to a few questions of a cultural nature. For example, we asked people to share a picture of their favourite local food. Sometimes this did not result in the national dish you would expect because some countries have very regional dishes. Then we asked them to share an activity in their country that they thoroughly enjoyed. Quite often, these were activities unique to that country and not something people did worldwide. The final question was to describe something very unique in their country. These presentations made the meeting both entertaining and educational.

The previous paragraph highlights one reason I came up with the term "cultural differences, human similarities." Everyone had something to equally share in terms of favourite dish, activity, and uniqueness. As well, they were all very proud of sharing things that were special to their country. These collective links are why I believe that it is not as challenging to manage a team that crosses cultures as some people think. I embrace the fact that there are cultural differences. I can deal with, and know, how to adjust to these differences. How is an adjustment possible? The bottom line is that all of these people are human, and what ties them together and makes it easier for me to deal with them is the human similarity.

When looking at different cultures on or outside your team, there are many shared links regardless of culture. Before reading the list that follows, close the book, and write down how you want to be treated at work. You can then open the book and see how many matches you have. From experience, I'm convinced that no matter where you live in the world, you will match at least half, if not more, of the items on this list. Again, you can overcome cultural differences by managing based on human similarities of shared desires such as:

- Everyone wants to be treated with respect
- They all want to know that you are effectively listening to them
- Everyone wants to be appreciated
- They all want to know that you care about their welfare
- Everyone is looking to be dealt with fairly and equally
- They all want to see that you have their back
- Everyone looks for you to be willing to support their development
- They all want to know that they can trust you
- Everyone wants to be thought of and treated as a person, not a resource
- They all want to pay their bills and take care of their families

There's an excellent chance that you came up with even more links than I've listed. If so, give it some thought as to whether this could apply to people across all cultures. If it does, send it to me, and I'll add it to the list!

The other apparent item is that cultures do not determine the ability of people either positively or negatively. You should certainly never judge any individual based on stereotypes as well. For example, don't assume they have superior math skills just because they come from a particular country. The previous topic of unconscious or conscious bias should reinforce this fact. I've met people from all over the world who are brilliant, they're fantastic human beings, and

I've been delighted to know them and work with them. I've also met people from all over the world that are lazy, careless, and not the kind of person you would want as a friend or neighbour. I'm sure all of you can agree on those statements. This reality says that cultural differences shouldn't mean anything regarding hiring or leading people because you should do so based on human similarities. After all, cultural differences aren't just across countries, but within countries as well. Here in Canada, there are cultural differences with ethnicity, or whether you grew up in a maritime province, in Quebec, in Toronto versus rural Ontario, raised on the prairies or cattle county or out on the west coast. Most Canadians are very similar, but some exhibit and operate with a cultural difference or bias.

Working with people from different cultures can open your world. You can discover many things about other places without even having to visit them. I feel that the acceptance of cultural differences helps support and build the 'flexible curiosity mindset' that you need to become more successful and satisfied. Then, if you model and share this acceptance and flexibility with your children (should you have any), it will just set them up for incredible success and satisfaction in their future.

CHAPTER 5

LEVEL 2 THINKING

I've separated these topics into a different level of thinking as they are typically in play with more people than the previous set. For example, while not many people utilize Six Sigma thinking, everyone multitasks!

Project Planning

Given the expansive scope of some projects and all the different documentation requirements, project planning has full-time roles. These roles are typically filled by someone trained and certified in project management. This section is not for project managers (PM) but for people who could benefit from using what I call a "project management light" process. Something a lot less than a PM needs to handle. A similar approach can aid us at home as well. All of us use these skills to a degree, but I know it's better if you can more consciously use some PM tools rather than hope that everything works out eventually.

The overall goal is to have everything completed by the initially agreed deadline plus on or below budget. To accomplish a PM needs to set up several things before the project work even starts. They need to ensure that there are well-documented objectives and that all stakeholders are agreed. Then working with those who need to execute, the PM must create a project plan with steps, responsible party, deadline and establish which steps are dependent upon others. She will also start a Risk Log for potential issues assumed at this time. As well, there needs to be an approved budget established. Finally, the PM needs to ensure that all resources, both in terms of people and materials, will be available as required. Sharing this at a kick-off meeting gets everyone on the same page with the plan.

Once the project starts, the PM needs to monitor progress daily plus, typically, a weekly meeting with key project members. They can report the status of each step and confirm that deadlines are still feasible. At this time, the members can also share any modifications to the Risk Log. The group should even agree on the overall project status, which is also known by the acronym RAG. The acronym starts with Red if there are severe problems and the team might need significant support from senior leaders to address the issues. Then it's Amber if there are some looming concerns around timings and risks. Finally, and hopefully, it's Green because everything is moving along according to plan. The PM communicates these items in a weekly status report to senior leaders. For a positive slant, the update should include "wins" from the past week. To recognize even small wins certainly helps with motivation and momentum.

As I said earlier, this section is not for anyone currently operating as a PM as I would be "preaching to the choir." I'm not expecting you to start creating risk logs or status reports or things like that if you're not a PM. That is unless you realize that they will help you. However, I do recommend that you undertake some project management light activities as follows:

1. Create a plan with all the steps needed and due dates for everything. You may have to do this in a right-to-left thinking way if the due date is already determined
2. Create a GANTT Chart, as you will see shortly, to visualize your project
3. Do make a list of all the resources you'll need for the project in terms of people, tools, and funds, and make sure you will have everything when needed
4. Review your progress weekly, but also decide your RAG status and react accordingly
5. Don't forget to celebrate your small wins
6. When you complete the project, have a more significant celebration because you've earned it

To give you a real example of project management light, I'll share the high-level project planning I did for this book. This will give you an idea of how this approach can keep you on track. For starters, a key objective was to have the book on the market by the time the Christmas gift-buying season started. Here's how my planning went using right-to-left thinking:

- To have the book available for the Christmas buying season, I used Black Friday in the US, November 27 this year, as the latest launch point.

Win It, Drive It!

- I need to finalize pricing by November 20, so researching competitive prices needs to start on November 13
- Knowing that Amazon needs a few days to approve a book for launch means getting it submitted into the system by November 18 to be safe
- November 13 is the date by which I want my final, edited draft review completed
- I am outsourcing the creation of the cover, which I want to be finalized by November 13, so I need to get the request into the company by November 9
- By November 6, I need to have completed the book description plus determined book dimensions, identified theme and target audience
- September 25 is when I need my 2nd draft completed
- August 18 is when the 1st draft needs to be completed
- With a goal of approximately 57,000 words for the 1st draft and a daily target of 1,500 words, by writing five days per week, I needed to start the book by June 24, which I did! (In case you're trying to do the math, I also excluded statutory holidays as that's time for the family!)

You can put these dates and steps into an Excel file and create a GANTT Chart like a PM. The chart for my plan is below:

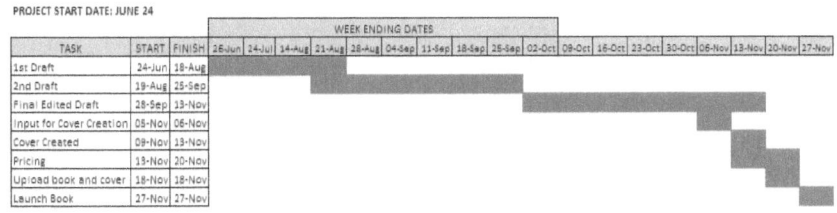

* Note: Some early weeks missing from chart purely to make it more readable

As an on-going visual reminder, you can print your GANTT Chart and post it up where you're working. Or you can put each of the deadlines into a calendar app with advanced notifications included to remind you at the right frequency and timing. Use whatever works for you to keep on top of things.

It won't be necessary for me to create a risk log. Most of the work is in my hands to complete, for starters, and I will be disciplined enough to make this happen. Secondly, for the work that others need to manage (cover creation and Amazon approval), I've built in buffer time in case it takes longer than they estimate. I do have one major risk, though, that is entirely out of my hands. I know this potential risk as it's a problem with my first book.

Before publishing the book, I can order an author's proof copy. You can use this copy as a final quality control step. Here you make sure that the pictures look good, spacing is correct for picture placement, plus one final spelling and grammar check. No matter where you live, your initial set up of the book is done through a system within Amazon in the US. When I put through an order for the proof, Amazon said they couldn't ship it to me. Due to COVID-19, they would only ship essential items internationally, and an author's proof was not considered essential. This rule made sense to me, and I was disappointed because all my momentum suddenly came to a stop. The circumstance was an unforeseen risk to my plan. I now needed to think about any mitigation options, so I contacted Amazon again. I asked, "When the book is published it can be purchased through Amazon Canada. So, could you not get that office to print the author's proof and ship it to me domestically?" The answer was, "No, proofs can only be printed in the US." My lateral thinking now kicked in to determine another mitigation option. I went back to Amazon again and asked, "Would you ship the proofs to a US address?" The answer was, "Sure, no problem." I then contacted a former colleague at Nielsen based in Green Bay, and she agreed to receive then send the proofs to me via the mail system. Once again, it looked like the plan was back in motion. Two days later, Cheryl received the proofs, and three days after that, the tracking system let me know the package was sent to Canada via Chicago. However, here it is 17 days later, and the box is still sitting at Canada Customs. As the pandemic has closed stores, shipping volumes have increased overwhelmingly, so delays are understandable. So, now I check the tracking each day and hope it will make it through soon. In the meantime, I need to add this as a risk to this book achieving its launch date. Perhaps I can use the actual receipt time of the author's proof as a benchmark for shipping time if COVID-19 keeps the situation the same two months from now.

A few days after I wrote the paragraph above, my first book finally arrived. In doing another quality check, some things jumped out in the book that weren't readily apparent when viewing the same material on a computer. Now comes decision time, which you can work through in your mind as you read. After making the changes, should another author's copy be ordered for a final check? The dilemma here is another three-week delay. In some ways, this isn't a problem as there's no commitment on a launch date. However, it would be valuable to get the book released soon for two reasons:

1. It would provide experience with launching a book, marketing, and getting feedback from reviews. All these things are helpful for this second book. There's a lot to learn, and the sooner this happens, the better.
2. At the end of the first book, I highlighted that this second book was underway. So, the more people reading the first book, the more who can be looking for this one before it's even released.

It seems that I'm at a crossroads. There's wanting to launch the book a.s.a.p. versus seeing it in final form before releasing, which means a three-week wait. What do you think I should do?

Remember, I asked Amazon if they could print my author's copy from Canada, and they said no? The fact is that, once I publish the book, they will print it in Canada for anyone who buys it there. As I did so many times in my career, I created a "workaround." Chances were excellent that everything was fine now. There should be no problem, then, with publishing the book. However, to conduct another quality check, I would order a book from Amazon Canada on the release day. With Prime service, it would arrive the very next day. I can then immediately unpublish the book, do the checks, upload any fixes, and then publish again. The downside is that if anyone else buys the book that same day, they won't have the minor amendments. Apologies if that happened, but it certainly wouldn't take away from the story or surprise ending.

The scenario above shows where lateral thinking or brainstorming can really come in handy because sh*t always happens. It's also an example of what will happen a lot at work. Perfection is great, but you shouldn't avoid or delay things waiting for perfection to happen. As the great American football coach Vince Lombardi once said, "Perfection is not attainable. But if we chase perfection, we can catch excellence." At times, then, you just need to move forward, do your temperature checks, or re-evaluate and adjust as needed. If you're sitting there on the side of the highway, everyone is passing you.

With "project management light," you do not do everything a PM would, but there's one crucial component to keep in mind. Namely, that there are three elements involved in projects, and they <u>must all stay in balance</u>. These elements are Scope, Time, and Resource (finance, people, and materials). They must be evaluated in tandem, and if a balance does not exist, you must adjust somewhere.

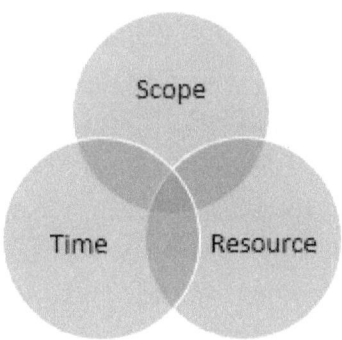

The first step is always defining the Scope. What is it that you, or your client, needs to get done? Is there a hard date (Time) by which you must finish the project? If yes, then use right-to-left thinking to see if available Resources can start when needed. It may be that one or two people starting tomorrow won't get it done. Then, do you have the capacity to begin a little later with a team of three? Or do you start with two people now and then add a third later in the project? In terms of other types of Resources, do you have the funds required and the equipment that three people will need? If there isn't a hard date set, look at the Resource element to determine the Time it will take to complete. Should that date not be acceptable, you then need to loop back and look at Resource options.

Eventually, you will determine the number of people needed, by when, and confirm that all the resources will be available to deliver the entire Scope by the agreed deadline. Great! However, a month into the project, the client says that, based on recent meetings, they need to increase the Scope. Now you need to sit down and assess whether this will impact Time or Resources, or both! If extending the Time is not an option, can you add the necessary people to the project and get the extra equipment they need? If that's possible, then you create an addendum to the contract to cover the additional cost, and away you go. If that's not possible, you're at a point where you need to deliver the project incrementally.

Incremental delivery is where "chunking" comes into play. It's a great tool to use in a variety of situations. If the client needs the Scope to increase, and there is no way possible to get Time and Resource to balance, chunking can help. What do I mean by that? I'll give you an example from my career where I was handed a project without any pre-sales input or assessment asked of me. The Scope required the creation of data extracts from over 700 databases. During the sell-in process, to get the client's signature, sales set an expectation that we could complete the work in six months. After the client signed everything, sales told me the Scope and the Time to deliver. The next step, then, was for me to calculate the Resource piece and ensure a balance. It worked out that I couldn't get enough Resources to deliver the entire Scope within the pre-determined Time. Compounding the Resources issue was that the client had assigned only two people on their side to work within the process. As a result, it didn't matter if we couldn't create all the extracts within that Time because they certainly couldn't keep up with us! If this story is ringing a bell, that's because it's one of the projects highlighted in the Six Sigma section.

In highlighting this to the client, I asked about priorities. If we, which included them, couldn't process everything by their originally anticipated deadline, let's chunk out the project by a priority list. At a high level, we first put "super-categories" in priority order. The next step was to determine the priority of individual categories within a super-category. We then had multiple milestone deadlines based on these priorities. The client was okay to accept this plan based on their Resource restrictions. In this case, the Scope stayed static, and the

Resource couldn't increase, so the project was segmented into chunks based on priorities to create multiple Times to deliver and keep a balance.

One final thought. Some people may have skipped this section, thinking they don't need to know anything about project management. Others may have read to this point and think they don't have the time to handle the steps I've suggested. Hopefully, you're not either of these people. When you've got something important to do, at work or home, with lots of moving parts, take the time to map out the project. It's guaranteed to save you considerable time and trouble and can be a tool to motivate you to keep going. Rest assured that people who try to save time by not planning will spend more time on the project when timings don't align, or things are overlooked. They're also frustrated throughout the whole exercise.

Time Management

One constant about time management is that no matter what you need to add or cut, no matter how much one day differs from the next – there are only 24 hours in a day. Unlike a project where time can shift, the number of hours in a day **never** changes. As with many of the topics I cover, there are entire books dedicated to this one. If time management is something you need to improve on, then buy one of those books. They're available on Amazon, and you can pay up to $70 for this one topic.

For our purposes, though, the information here is designed to give you awareness, at a high level, of what you should incorporate into your skill set. Even if you feel you know what "time management" means, this information will give you a different way to think about this skill. For example, some people think of time management just in terms of their job, but it should be in terms of your entire day. This approach is particularly true, where you have the approval to manage a work/life balance that works for you.

One of the essential elements of time management is the ability to say "no." I've found that many people who are always in scramble mode have two problems. The first is that they do not actively manage their time. The second is that they never say no to requests and get overloaded with tasks and conflicting deadlines. The challenge is that human nature makes us all like to help people when asked. However, we need to do a better job at considering, through time management, whether we can handle the request. And maybe the "no" is just for now, which can be turned into a "yes" in a few months when things get cleared off your plate.

Demands on your time will increase as you climb higher in an organization. The number of times you have to say "no" will increase as well. How do these successful people decide when to say "no?" They always keep their goals in mind. If the request is something that does not apply to their goals, they say "no." They hold firm to their plans because their goals create success. Anything that would distract or take away from accomplishing their goals is easy to turn down. I've also noticed that they genuinely control their time. Trying to meet with them must be at their convenience timewise, even if it's inconvenient for you. As well, your meeting can easily get bumped should something more critical to their goals now conflict with your timing. They are not being mean, just managing their time aligned with goals and priorities as we all should.

Time management is about <u>consciously</u> controlling what you're working on and when. It includes several factors, such as:

- Knowing your goals

- Understanding your priorities
- Project planning skills (due dates, time estimates, doing things concurrently vs. consecutively)
- Ability to work in an efficient, undistracted way
- Balancing what you need to do at work and in your personal life
- Holding firm against your plans

Regarding this topic, I must mention the insightful book "Deep Work" by Cal Newport (Newport, 2016). The reason being, there are essential elements in Cal's book that apply to all of us no matter our role or company or industry. The first one is that when we portion out our 24 hours each day, there must be a 3 to 4-hour chunk for "deep work." This term is related to innovation and problem-solving, those things that can make an impactful difference for ourselves and others. The second element is that you must allocate time to "shallow work," which are things like checking a social media app to see a picture of your friends' lunch, checking emails we didn't need to receive...

Cal highlights that to create more time for deep work, which has value and purpose, you can eliminate many things on the shallow side, such as social media apps. These things are fun and exciting, but they don't give you the return on investment for the time you spend on them. As mentioned earlier, <u>time is finite</u> each day. You can spend it wisely or waste it away. That's not to say that you need to be ignoring anything fun or exciting. It's to highlight that you must manage your time wisely, so the right amount is allocated to those things needed to move you onwards. Rest assured, you will still have time each day for fun things. They merely need to be appropriately time managed.

There are many ways to handle time management. At the high end, you could look to schedule every part of every day. However, I know this is something that very few people will be able to, or even want to, achieve. If you can schedule every part of every day, then go right ahead. Do it, and congratulations to you! If, however, you can't do this or most of your time is already blocked off by meetings and calls, do yourself a favour and at least schedule time for deep work. Then, to support that schedule, **never** let yourself get distracted by the shallow work of social media, instant messaging, or pop-up emails!

If this still seems like something overwhelming or not what you like doing, try it in a small, controlled way. I hope you have created one or more SMART goals for yourself already. If so, then try a time management technique with one. Knowing your completion date, map out when you're going to work on it. Then, in those scheduled blocks of time, make sure you approach this time like "deep work." Shut off your email, phone, and social media apps, close the door and focus 100% on what you need to do. When you've completed your SMART goal, reflect on how things went and whether using this time management approach helped your productivity, quality, and creativity.

As with anything new, take baby steps, then as you get comfortable and confident, stretch yourself further. Keep doing this in incremental stages, and before long, you'll be amazed at your level of improvement. Time is finite and precious, so manage it wisely.

Dangers of Multitasking

Standard and dangerous opinions are that you can accomplish more by multitasking. Unfortunately, while most people believe this, there's significant evidence to the contrary. The steadily increasing amount of work and constant deadlines has pushed people to multitask, thinking that this helps them stay on top of everything. Globalization has now greatly extended the number of hours each day where people can receive an email, which compounds the issue. Many emails from Asia hit my inbox in the middle of the night while I was sleeping. As well, communication overload has increasingly become worse over the years due to technology. Nowadays, there are multiple ways for the same people to communicate with one another. People can now be reached anytime, anywhere globally, through various applications on their smartphones. In the not-so-distant past, if I were driving on the highway anywhere at 10 am, you'd have to wait until I got to my destination and hope I was near a landline. While driving these days, I can hear my phone ping when receiving the email just sent to me. Then it pings again because the same person just sent an instant message to see if I've read their email. Then the car alerts me that there's a phone call connecting to its system via Bluetooth. That person is now calling to see if I've seen the instant message about the email they sent. Guess I better click the answer option so I can talk to this person while driving.

Does my car scenario illustrate how technology impacts our work-life sound exactly like what happens to you every day? Well, talking to someone over your phone (handsfree of course, as that's the safest way) is not really what I'm talking about in terms of multitasking. However, it does illustrate how multiple technology tools have morphed more people into multitasking on the job. People let themselves get dragged into multitasking by allowing all these tools into play simultaneously during their workday. Sadly, there's even more technology, like social media apps, that add to the distraction.

How I define multitasking and its' dangers on the job is: "Attempting to work on critical and valuable tasks while simultaneously having open, and available, multiple applications and distractions which will slow down productivity and impede your ability to deliver optimal results."

The next time you're at work, see if this scenario applies to you:

Task:

You have a proposal that needs to get out to your client tomorrow. Competitors are pitching to your client for the same work.

Situation:

- You have the document open and need to determine price, projected delivery dates by your operations group, and terms of the agreement
- The instant message app on your computer pops up a few times, and you stop to read those messages and perhaps reply
- Email notifications pop up regularly. You quickly glance at the message to see who it's from and the topic. Most of the time, you'll ignore the email, but sometimes you'll open it up to read the content
- You have your Internet browser open, and there are multiple tabs active with things like weather, Gmail, news, and Facebook. Occasionally your mind gets you to check these tabs for anything new
- Your smartphone sits next to your computer. While you're working on the proposal, apps like Messenger and Snapchat 'ping' a few times. Of course, you quickly check what has been sent only to find that it's a picture of a friends' lunch! You also looked at two text messages from friends about plans for next week

Here you need to complete a critical document, and while working on it, you've been distracted more than a dozen times. Still, you believe that you're productive because you're working on your proposal, checking your instant messages and emails all at the same time. Plus, why does it matter that you're also checking all those personal items, you're still going to finish the proposal today?

You may think that multitasking is not truly a problem because you got the proposal completed plus checked your emails, instant messages, texts, snaps, and Facebook feed. All in a days' work. Your next thought could be, "Why would he say dangers?" Learnings from a neuroscience perspective are the reason for the word danger. Neuroscientists have conducted extensive studies over the years to measure the impact of multitasking on the brain. They have the tools and the ability to measure brainwaves to compare the effect, on the brain, of those people multitasking as described above versus someone who is 100% focused on only writing the proposal.

A study by the University of Sussex (UK) proved that over a long period of time, the constant distractions you get from technology could alter your brain structure (1).

A neuroscientist at MIT found that our brains have a limitation on resources and energy. We also have a minimal capacity to hold simultaneous thought. Therefore, switching back and forth between a proposal and emails uses up some of this resource capacity. This switching dilutes your creative ability for the proposal. Yes, you got it done, but it <u>wasn't your best work</u>. (2)

Here is one danger I started to succumb to in the past year and am now working to control. According to neuroscientist and New York

Times best-selling author Daniel Levitin, "Multitasking creates a dopamine-addiction feedback loop, effectively rewarding the brain for losing focus and for constantly searching for external stimulation." (3)

Levitin suggests that the brain regions that need to stay focused on a task are also easily distracted. By multitasking, we train our brains to lose the valuable focus we need on some jobs by getting distracted with other things. Unfortunately, our brain can get addicted to not focusing on one thing as it's hard work to concentrate. Therefore, like an addiction to a drug, your brain is continuously enticing you to multitask as a reward. This reward cycle can be challenging to break!

It's fair to say that this kind of addiction is easy to spot in others as well. It's visible when people are walking on the street, looking at their phones rather than anything around them. Or maybe they keep glancing at their phone while you're trying to have a conversation with them. At the office, you might be sitting at their desk, having a conversation. Still, their head turns to their computer screen every time they hear a 'ping.' It's like we have all become Pavlov's dogs; our brains conditioned to become distracted with every ping or pop-up box on our phones and computers.

If you're not familiar with Pavlov's dogs, Google it to see how these stimuli can be trained into our brains. Then take some time to

(1) Ryota et al (2014). Higher media multitasking activity is associated with smaller gray-matter density in the anterior cingulate cortex
(2) Janssen et al. Integrating knowledge of multitasking and interruptions across different perspectives and research methods.
(3) Junco et al (2012). No A 4 U: The relationship between multitasking and academic performance

self-reflect and see if this is something that often happens to you. LOL: My phone just 'pinged,' and I had to force myself not to look! See, I told you I was still working on overcoming this danger.

In trying to learn and multitasking, you will never be as smart as the training's potential. In other words, only by focusing 100% on the learning is your potential to leverage this new knowledge maximized. If you're stopping to check emails or text messages or looking at whatever during a learning session, you will probably only be able to leverage, say, 80% of the learning. With your brain switching back and forth between the teaching and the distractions, you'll lose 20%. Let's say that the trainer declares, "If you absorb everything I'm saying, I'll give you $100, but if you check email or look at an app during this time, I'll only give you $80." Would you pay attention or throw money away to see that picture of a friends' lunch instantly? Our brains cannot fully and comprehensively absorb multiple, disparate streams of information via multitasking. Operating in a distracted way reduces your potential!

Similarly, as much as multitasking hurts your potential for optimal learning, it also damages your ability to be creative and innovative. These processes require intense focus and concentration as their very essence relates to things currently unknown. There is nothing routine, historical, or easy about being creative or innovative. Why, then, do people think they can develop something new and unique while also jumping back and forth between mundane tasks?

So far, the dangers are reduced productivity and impeding your ability to learn to an optimal level. Then there's the impact on creativity and innovation. All these things will impact your performance. However, these dangers will not only affect your performance but your mental and physical health as well. Again, you can check with the neuroscientists on how multitasking impacts your brain specifically and medically if you want. Or you can agree that, most likely, multitasking has caused you stress and anxiety plus a sense of feeling overwhelmed and exhausted regularly.

We could accomplish more in the day if we were to portion out our work as focused chunks. For example, start the day by only checking your email first, then close it. Leave your phone in your desk or pocket and only "grab it when it rings, not when it pings." Don't have the Internet open unless you need to check something specifically for exactly what you're working on at that moment, then close it down.

I know everyone isn't a robot, and a little distraction can help during the day, but it still needs to be managed the right way. So, when you finish a specific task, you can take a little mental break by checking your apps. When the respite is over, put the phone away again, keep your email closed and start focusing on the next task.

Let's say two people are doing the same job, and they're precisely the same in terms of intelligence, knowledge, and experience. However, one difference is that the first one operates like a typical multitasker, whereas the second one tries to avoid multitasking and spends more time in full concentration (deep work). Based on the picture below, which person do you think would write a better proposal recognizing that they each spent exactly two hours on this task? Also, between the two, who do you think would feel more stressed and tired by lunchtime?

Win It, Drive It!

9:00	9:30	10:00	10:30	11:00	11:30
Check email	Check email	Check email	Check email	Check email	Check email
Write Proposal	Write Proposal	Write Proposal	Write Proposal	Write Proposal	Write Proposal
Answer IM		Answer IM	Answer IM		Answer IM
	Check Smartphone ping	Check Smartphone ping		Check Smartphone ping	Check Smartphone ping

9:00	9:30	10:00	10:30	11:00	11:30
Check email					Check email
	Write Proposal	Write Proposal	Write Proposal	Write Proposal	
					Answer IM
					Check Smartphone ping

Here's an ask from me. If you see yourself as the person currently operating in the top box, commit yourself to work as the person in the bottom for one week. See if it changes your stress level, sustains your energy longer, and helps you to complete things more efficiently. I know this will be difficult because long-term multitasking makes your brain crave being distracted. When moving from the top box to the bottom, your brain must focus, no more distractions. In both examples, the person is doing the same amount of work in the same timeframe. The only difference is multitasking versus focused work. It is highly feasible for you to work in a concentrated manner. If making this change is difficult, it's not because of your work; it's because your brain is craving the distractions it is no longer getting. This reaction should prove that multitasking is of no real value; in fact, it's quite dangerous for you.

If you want to learn more about improving your performance and value, which means focus versus distractions, please read Cal's book: "Deep Work: Rules for Focused Success in a Distracted World." He helps you to understand the definitions and differences of deep versus shallow work. A key difference is the increased extent of value to your success and happiness through deep work. Cal supports most of his recommendations by connecting them to what is understood through neuroscience, psychology, and philosophy. If you can consistently work in a deep way, and your competition mostly works the shallow (easy) way, you will win!

I can relate to what he shares for a few simple reasons. Firstly, I've experienced how shallow work has distracted me but not provided any value. The best example is email. I would receive hundreds of emails each week and never be able to get through them all. I would quickly glance at the content to see if something were required of me urgently. Usually, this wasn't the case as I was mostly on the 'CC' line, not the 'To' line. At times, seeing the number of unread emails would start to stress me. So, I would sit down on a Saturday and spend around 6 hours cleaning up the Inbox. As a check on the value of this time, I cleared out the Trash bin. At the end of the clean-up, I looked to see how many emails were now there. Then I calculated the percent versus what was in the Inbox when I started. I consistently calculated around 80% of emails that I reviewed that I didn't even need to see. This result means almost 5 hours of my time spent on shallow work that produced zero value for me. So, if I'm switching back and forth from valuable work to emails, the distraction through multi-tasking is hurting me while providing no value. Perhaps you should try this as a test someday soon and see if you get the same results.

The second element is that regularly checking these 'no value' emails or social media pop-ups has made my brain addicted to being distracted. I'm sure that most everyone is addicted as well, meaning they are chronically distracted. This creates a state of mind where you can't even wait somewhere for 5 minutes without checking your smartphone. Look around to see how many people can't go for a walk without constantly looking at their phone? Spend some time watching others. Are they sitting in front of the TV with a movie on, yet still looking down at their phone? Are they having a conversation with someone but looking at their phone and not at them? Self-reflection time! How many distractions have stopped you from the focused attention of reading and absorbing what is in this book?

Can we conclude, then, that constant multitasking makes you less efficient, less creative, reduces your ability to optimize learning, all while increasing stress, anxiety, and exhaustion? I say, "Yes!" What do you say?

Persuasion and Negotiation

Everyone needs to use these skills throughout their lifetimes, more so outside of the office than inside actually. We must persuade and negotiate with our spouses/partners, our children, or a car salesman. Unfortunately, I've never been overly successful with persuasion or negotiation with any of those people! These are valuable skills to add to your arsenal. Again, there are lots of books on the market dedicated to these topics. As usual, in this book's spirit, I provide an overview to add it to your overarching mindset.

You can think of persuasion and negotiation as two siblings. They are from the same family, but there are some differences. Persuasion involves that action or process to get someone to do something or believe in something. On the other hand, negotiation is a give-and-take situation where two parties try to arrive at a contractual agreement. Not always, but for the most part.

To me, it's easier to be successful in these two areas through your character and track record. It's much easier to persuade or negotiate when people know you're ethical, reliable, trustworthy, and always come through. Your character can also help at times when you're not even around. As an example, friends of mine were completing a move on a Sunday. I hadn't shown up after some time but had been there the full day on Saturday. One person questioned why I was so late. Based on knowing my character, another person said, "Marty would have been here already if he said he was coming today." This statement quickly closed out the first persons' question.

This is an excellent place to discuss reputation versus character. Many people think they are the same thing. You might think that my friends' conclusion was based on my reputation, not my character. While these two things are closely linked, there is a difference. Your reputation is what others think of you or has heard about you. Your reputation, then, can differ from one person to the next based on what they've heard or how well they truly know you. Your character, though, is your authentic essence, and it drives how you conduct yourself. Character is your true self, whereas reputation is from others' opinions, which may not be spot on. My friends' conclusion was based on knowing my character and not what my reputation might be with others.

The better that people know you, the easier it is to persuade them. Again, people know that I'm honest and look for win-win situations, to move things forward quite quickly. They don't hesitate to make decisions by first determining if they can trust the message. I've always said that I tell the truth for a few simple reasons. Firstly, it's just the right thing, the ethical thing to do. Secondly, it's effortless for me to remember the truth. When you tell lies, it can be hard to remember exactly how the lie went. Lying is where people get caught when their story starts to change. And once you get caught this way, it damages your character and reputation. Here's Warren Buffett's (7th richest person in the world) quote to keep in mind. "It takes 20 years to build a reputation and five minutes to ruin it. If you think about that, you'll do things differently."

Another way to think about this topic is from the flip side. What kinds of thoughts go through your head when someone is trying to persuade you or negotiate with you? Are you half listening to what they say while the other half of your brain assesses whether you can believe or trust this person? Here's another great quote from Warren Buffett in terms of hiring advice. "You need to ensure your new hires have integrity. All the skill in the world, but a lack of integrity, will lead to serious problems. Integrity is choosing your thoughts and actions based on <u>values</u> rather than personal gain." Can you be persuaded by or like being in a negotiation with someone who lacks integrity?

To be persuasive, you must create an emotional connection. This connection is enabled through a trust which you can generate by being authentic. And that authenticity needs to remain throughout the relationship. Again, like telling lies, if it appears that you have not been legitimate with the other party, there goes their trust replaced by damage to your character and reputation. Then, when they talk to other people, do you think they're recommending you to others or warning them about you? What kind of damage to your ability to network do you think that creates?

There's an excellent book available on this topic by Arlene Dickinson appropriately entitled "Persuasion." (Dickinson, 2011) If you want to improve in this area, this is an excellent book to read. One thing that struck me was that most of the content is common sense, yet people often don't use it. Some of it also related to topics in this book, with effective listening being a critical point. Common sense, how can you persuade someone if you're not listening effectively to them? As I have said about interviewing, it's really what the other person wants, not what you want. You need to focus on what they want so you can share the appropriate SOAR stories. It's also an essential element of her book that you should persuade through stories. This action engages your audience more interestingly and helps them remember what you've said. This fact is why I share many of my career and personal stories here. I also teach my students by sharing many of these same tales.

There was one critical nugget in her book that made me smile. Arlene states that you must believe what you're doing is valuable and worthwhile. By having this sense of self-worth and purpose, you can defend against rejection. This piece of advice has helped me move forward while writing this book. I genuinely believe it is invaluable to help people struggling to get a job or advance in their careers. This benefit is my version of, "what's in it for them?"

The other part of this topic is negotiation, of which persuasion is a significant subset. You can't have a successful negotiation if you're unable to persuade the other party. As mentioned earlier, negotiation is an essential skill at work and in your personal life. At work, you could be negotiating on several items, such as:

- Agreeing on the elements of an initial job offer in terms of starting salary, vacation time, or the ability to work from home
- Looking for a salary increase
- Trying to settle disputes between employees or departments
- Negotiating price and delivery times with a client or with a vendor when you're the client
- …

In our personal lives, we need strong negotiation skills when looking to buy a house or a car. Or maybe when you're involved in organizing a charitable event. The same degree of knowledge and skill is required, and the importance is just as great.

Although persuasion is a subset of negotiation, there are common elements, with the most important one being effective listening. As well, you must look to create a win-win situation. Obviously, the closer you can get to an ideal win-win, the faster you can conclude the negotiation. As with persuasion, you need to be asking great questions and digging into the subtext for the truth behind the other person's position. Sometimes they won't reveal why they're sticking their toes in the sand. Other times they've taken their stance without realizing your situation. The more you can move them from a 'them versus you' frame of mind to a place where they can be empathetic and look to converse in the sense of togetherness, the better.

You can't go through a career or life without the constant need for solid persuasion and negotiation skills. So, the more you can learn about these things, work on them and perfect them, the better off you and those you interact with will be.

CHAPTER 6

CONNECTING WITH OTHERS

Many people think that to have a successful career means that the vertical path should be narrow. An example of a narrow path is that they start in a junior sales rep role. Then over time, they move up to senior sales rep. Then up to district sales manager, then regional sales manager, then national. There is certainly nothing wrong with this as they demonstrated success over time. However, you can be just as successful, or maybe even more so, if you look to work in cross-functional assignments. One key benefit here is that it gives you a much broader perspective of the business. You get a real appreciation for the challenges faced by different groups, which helps develop empathy, creating better working relationships.

Moving around the business can also lead to more significant job and personal satisfaction as you are greatly expanding your skills, knowledge, and experiences. As mentioned, my career went from external auditor to internal operations roles, IT type role, sales, and service plus leadership roles, from a national to a global perspective. There was never a dull moment and believe me; I bore easily! The Nielsen Company also enabled working cross-functionally on a proactive basis. I can't say if they're still doing this now, but at one point, they were asking people to volunteer to swap departments for a year. The promise was that you were guaranteed your old job back in 12 months if that's what you wanted at that point. The benefits I saw were:

1. Multiple individuals gaining new knowledge and experiences and developing new skills
2. Departments getting fresh perspectives from talented people that were successful in their other roles
3. Other individuals would get to hear insights from the new people, in a cross-pollination kind of way

Another program at Nielsen that quantified the value of working cross-functionally, in my mind, was the Emerging Leaders Program (ELP). Young people who had excelled at university, and showed great promise early in their careers, were placed into this program for two years. During that time, they would have four rotations that would move them around the business. They were tasked with any problem-solving or new idea development as defined by the department. The department's work request had to be approved by the governing body for the program. If approved, it was added to a pool from which the ELP candidates would choose three requests of interest. Internal interviews would happen, and then the candidates would be assigned to a department for the next six months. As part of their training, it was necessary to present to the whole group after three months to show your objectives, results to date and plans over the remaining time. Then at the six-month mark, another presentation was necessary to deliver the concluding results of the assignment. A vital part of the final presentation was to share what the ELP candidate had gained in terms of new knowledge or skills.

Even if your company doesn't do something like this, I think this program shows the real value for you to move around cross-functionally and build a comprehensive business knowledge. It will open so many extra doors for you to pick and choose where you want to go.

What does this have to do with the topic of connecting with others? When you work in different areas, it helps you connect with others in an empathetic way, as "you've been in their shoes." It makes conversations more manageable and robust as you have a better understanding of their area. It also makes you more willing to have a deeper connection. Unfortunately, I've heard a lot of unproductive and dysfunctional conversations over the years. The situations have been during critical talks between different departments. There would be client-facing people thinking that the operations staff was beneath them. That, as client-facing, they were 100% responsible for the success of the company.

Conversely, there would be operations people who thought that client-facing staff had an easy and fun time at work. Having worked on both sides, I found that the job was challenging for both sides in different ways. Both sides worked long hours and were committed to doing their best to drive client satisfaction. Some people, though, just couldn't connect with others in different groups, and it just made their job more difficult for that reason alone.

Hopefully, you will have the opportunity to work in different areas of a business. This will help you to connect more deeply with others. Let's now look at more valuable ways in which to associate with others through:

1. Effective Listening
2. Team Player and Teamwork
3. Networking
4. Mentoring
5. Remotely Managed

Effective Listening

Something I still remember from grade school was a simple demonstration of communication skills. One key element was each persons' ability to listen effectively. There is a good chance you played this game in your youth as well. It was called "Chinese whispers." If you don't know this game, this is how it unfolded. The teacher had all students stand up next to their desks. Then she would whisper a short story into the ear of each student in the first row. Those students would then turn and whisper it to the classmate in the row behind them. This would continue until all the students in the last row had heard the story. Those students would then share what they heard to compare to the teacher's original story. The challenge was to see if the last student correctly shared the entire, original story. However, this was usually a funny exercise, as no one got their story correct. The more incorrect the tale, the more all the students laughed. The main lesson in this game was that messages could become wrong through a lack of effective listening skills.

Optimal verbal communication requires a robust two-way process. The perfect verbal message is diluted if, on the receiving end, the other person is not listening effectively. On the other side of the coin, effective listening can determine if the verbal message is less than perfect. Not all the time, mind you, but you can pick up if specific details are missing or the directive is becoming mixed if you are listening effectively. This reason is why I believe that of the two pieces of transmitting a message, listening skills are far more critical.

The best listeners are active, not passive, in that they are genuinely focused on understanding the message. To optimize focus means that while listening, you are not trying to formulate a response. As Stephen R Covey said, "Most people do not listen with the intent to understand; they listen with the intent to reply." Would you not agree that your brain has a reduced ability to understand what it's hearing if it's engaged in formulating a response? If you catch yourself doing this instead of listening, it would be best to confirm what you have understood by relaying back to the speaker what you heard. If the listener doesn't confirm, it's an excellent step for the speaker to ensure the receiver understood. How many times have you given verbal instructions, not asked for a confirmation of understanding, then found out that they did not follow your instructions? This outcome usually results in a later conversation where the receiver says, "Well this is what I heard." It's too bad that they hadn't previously verbalized their understanding of the instructions.

Effective listening will also require you, at times, to listen without going into a defensive mode. Doing so can come into play at work during your annual review when you're getting difficult feedback. It may also need to kick in at a client meeting or when things are going wrong at work, and the managers are looking for someone to blame! Some criticism and difficult feedback are not particularly warranted. It can come from people who are managers by default, or unreasonable clients, or people looking to deflect blame from themselves. In these situations, you must actively and effectively, without being in a defensive mode, listen to the message to pick out whether this difficult feedback is valid or not. If it's accurate, then you need to do something to ensure you don't need to hear this kind of feedback again. If it's not valid, then you need to take different steps. By the way, listening without going into a defensive mode at home is massively beneficial! It's just as challenging to hear difficult feedback there as it is at work.

Effective listening gets enhanced through your observational skills. Sometimes the message doesn't match the speakers' demeanour. Sometimes, based on what you observe in the speaker, you need to ask them questions to dig deeper. Why? Many people who need to give difficult feedback are afraid to provide this type of message. They try to soften it, so you don't get mad at them. Or sometimes they're upset about something else but taking it out on you. Is the issue being discussed the real problem, or does body language say there's something else lurking in the background?

Observational skills are also essential if you're the one that is having to give difficult feedback to someone else. Are they listening in a non-defensive mode, or can you notice that they've got their back up and are not absorbing anything you're saying? If their back is up, then this is a one-way conversation meaning it's ineffective at this point. The purpose is to correct or improve behaviour, attitude, and performance, so the conversation needs to be two-ways. If the feedback is valid, then it's for the other persons' benefit, and they need to be listening to understand.

A little earlier, we looked at the skill of persuasion. Key suggestions to improve your performance in that area were that you needed to create emotional connections, listen for sub-text, and ask great questions to build on the conversation. None of those requirements are possible without effective, focused, and connected listening. We can all tell when someone isn't listening to us. Does this create or break an emotional connection? When someone relates an incorrect understanding of your message, you know when it's due to them not listening effectively. And sometimes, when people claim they didn't understand, it's not because of an inability to understand; they just didn't listen intently. Isn't that frustrating as well? Have you ever shouted "Listening skills" to your children because you knew they weren't paying attention to your message?

Practical listening skills are essential for everyone. In terms of leadership, which is covered later, listening includes the "Willingness to be influenced by subordinates." Listening to this level is a characteristic of a servant leader who is someone great to work for. They recognize that they may not be the smartest person in the room and can learn something valuable from others. They also know Kenneth Blanchard's quote that I like to remind people about; "None of us is as smart as all of us." The further people stray from these last two points; the more ineffective is their listening skill. Primarily because they don't believe they need to listen carefully. Remind you of any specific leaders during the global pandemic?

Networking

Many people simply come into the office in the morning, work at their desk for 8 hours, then go home. They do this week after week, month after month and year after year. Then, they wonder, "Why am I going nowhere? Why are the people around me getting promotions or new jobs?" Then others put in more effort but also have the same questions. They get more exasperated because they show up every day and work harder than those who leave after 8 hours. They believe that just showing up every day and working hard is enough on its' own. While doing this is "<u>to expectation</u>," it's never going to be enough. Why? That's because other people also show up every day and work hard but take the extra step of networking.

No surprise but, there are tons of books available that are devoted exclusively to networking. That's because it's a useful skill to have. If you want your career to take off, it will be worth buying one of those books. Until then, here are some thoughts on networking to add as part of your bigger picture. However, before talking about what networking is, let's cover what it is not. Networking is not things like:

- Sucking up to your boss
- Booking coffees or lunches with executives to brag to your peers
- Asking people to find you a job
- Asking for help without expecting to reciprocate
- Running around, handing out hundreds of business cards
- Asking for 'dirt' on other people

Networking is the process of interacting with other people to exchange information and develop professional or social contacts. The most critical word in that sentence is exchange. You must always engage in networking as a two-way street. If you think it's a one-way street for you, then you'll find a dead-end at some point soon. If you expect to get a lot out of networking, you need to put much effort into it for others.

LinkedIn (LI) is the best business networking tool in the world. Over 706 million members spread across 200+ countries testify to that statement. I've been a member for around 20 years (www.linkedin.com/in/martylateralthinkerdupuis) and have used this tool in many ways. It's helped me to stay connected with work colleagues who moved onto other companies. I've learned a lot of tips and tricks by reading articles that people post. You can hear from some of today's great business authors like Dr. Travis Bradberry, Brenè Brown, and Adam Grant. Like me, you can follow them on LI and get a regular dose of their excellent advice and motivations. I've also taken a lot of the training courses available on the website. You can get access by either subscribing to LI premium service or, hopefully, work for a company that subscribes on behalf of their employees.

In life, we should always be looking to give to others. So, this should make the exchange part of networking easy for us. As I was getting something from being a LI member, I wanted to give back through the platform. Therefore, as mentioned in the beginning, I signed up to be an advisor. In short order, I saw six people whose thought process and approach needed work. They posted a simple advice request and expected others to do all the hard work to find them jobs! Let's look at a few examples of these real people looking for help through posting these actual questions.

Request: "Opportunities where my experience would be an asset." This person is basically asking you to go from this page to her profile, read and analyze her experience and skills, then come up with a list of job openings or related jobs and let her know. As you can see, you would be doing the heavy lifting here. This request doesn't lend itself to being easy to support in a 'request and advice message' format as enabled on LI.

Request: "All advice is welcome." A project manager wrote this ask. Perhaps I should have responded by asking him to determine which <u>actionable</u> question he wanted to have answered? What was he expecting to hear back? For your information, this person, and the one above, are both currently employed. What kind of return on investment do you think their current employers are getting from them?

Request: "Whatever pays the bills." This statement, not a question, was submitted by a student still attending college. Like the people above, they had put no real thought into the request. If they don't know where they genuinely want to go, how would you know? Would you like to advise or hire someone who has no real direction for themselves?

When you are looking for guidance or help to find a job, there are a few things to remember:

1. It would be best if you were doing the heavy lifting in knowing yourself and what you're looking for
2. Your request needs to be as specific as possible. Not wide open like the ones above
3. Whoever is helping you, their time is valuable, so nail the first two points to take up the least amount of their time

Another person currently in college sent me a connection request and the following message (I have copied the request verbatim. Name and city not provided to protect their identity):

"My name is …, I am into marketing management course. I am finding a a job from several months but could not able to find it because I don't have any references here at …, so please help me finding a job. Thank you"

There were a few things that troubled me with this request, namely:

1. They have not proof-read their request.
2. You will notice that the sentence structure is not correct. However, I know that English is not this person's native language, so I cut them a little slack there.
3. They haven't put much effort into the request nor plotted it out for a good communication flow. The basic message is, "I'm in school, please help me find a job."

However, I responded and asked questions to get a better fix on what he was looking for. He answered and sent his resume this time. I then provided him with five pieces of advice to support his search.

Two months later, he replied with the same request, "Please help me find a job." This time I asked one question, "Did you follow any of the advice I provided previously?" He never responded to this query. He's probably still sitting at home, without a job, and wondering why he can't find anything. He's probably also blaming society for his situation.

Networking can come in many different forms. There are one-to-one meetings with people. Then there are industry conventions where you can meet several people in a single day. The common thread is that you're meeting more people, and more people are getting to know you. It's about continuing to expand your network. However, it's not only to create more connections just for you. Authentically it would be best if you were looking to make connections between other people to help them. When you're authentic about networking, without "selling yourself," you are genuinely selling yourself on the road to career success, professional growth, and personal satisfaction.

An excellent networking opportunity is with any cross-functional department projects. These allow you to learn about other business areas, meet new people and get them to know you. Please don't be afraid to put your hand up if it's a demanding or potentially problematic project. The benefit to you can outweigh the challenges. When these opportunities pop up, many people, particularly non-team players, keep their heads down. They worry that they're not up to the challenge, will struggle or fail and therefore think it will hurt future advancement opportunities. To me, they've got their thinking reversed! Leaders notice and remember those that don't offer to step up. Leaders also know that the project is a challenge, things may stumble along, and you will encounter problems. They look at people who volunteer for these challenges and work through the issues, even if they struggle at times, as the kind of people they want to promote. If you want your career to stall or stay that way, just keep your head down. If you desire to advance, take on these difficult challenges and appreciate that they will help you network while further developing critical skills like tenacity, problem-solving, and optimism.

Here are some simple questions for you regarding networking. The first is whether, or not, you have a profile on LinkedIn. If you don't, then put it in your calendar to create as soon as possible. Even if you're a student and may not have much to put on regarding work experience, get started now. LI is a tool that you will use for business networking for years to come. The sooner you get on there and start seeing what's shared, promoted and discussed, the better.

If you do have a LinkedIn profile, how satisfied are you with your utility of this tool? If you have many connections, do you regularly check the site and, at times, post comments? If you have a bare-bones profile and haven't been on the site for months, block time in your calendar, and build up your profile and connections. LI is there for everyone's benefit, and there's extensive value for you to gain. However, don't just create a profile and then think that someone will magically reach out to offer you a premium job. Like everything of value in life, you're only going to get out what you put in.

Team Player and Teamwork

You may wonder why I've included a team player as a topic. You might be thinking, "This isn't necessary because everyone knows you need to work as a team." Trust me, over the years, I've seen enough people that weren't team players and intentionally avoided teamwork. No surprise, then, that none of them were ever very successful. Your next question might be, "What do you mean by avoid?" These people and there were not lots of them, never put their hand up to volunteer for anything. They never asked if any of their teammates needed help with anything. At times they were directly asked if they would help, and these people would come up with some excuse as to why they couldn't. They only wanted to do the minimum needed for their job and nothing more. They would congratulate themselves for working in this kind of "stealth mode." They thought that no one noticed, but everyone noticed! For sure, their boss noticed, so guess who didn't get offered any new opportunities or promotions? Sadly, some of these people even got upset that they were passed over for a promotion and thought that the whole world was against them.

I've used the terms team player and teamwork. You may think that they're the same, but they're not, and it's valuable to know the difference. For example, someone can participate in teamwork but not be a team player. Teamwork is, in essence, an efficient and effective way in which a group performs together. Being a team player can mean things like sacrificing for others, giving credit where credit is due, and having an awareness of others. As a team player, you never look for opportunities to try and put yourself above others. Your thoughts and efforts are focused on total team success and not your success. You can have ten people on a team working together (teamwork), with some going the extra mile to support others (team player) and others not pulling their weight. Just because someone is on a team and participating in teamwork doesn't necessarily mean they are a team player. These things get noticed!

The nature of being a team player is very consistent in its' form. On the other hand, the essence of teamwork has many forms. Most people think this only applies to the team or group you belong to at work, but working as a team extends to other conditions such as:

- With your boss
- On any cross-functional department projects
- In representing your company externally
- With your client and their team
- In personal settings like sports teams or charitable organizations

Contributing to teamwork as a team player is accomplished in a variety of ways:

- Knowing your role and excelling in it
- Sacrificing when necessary
- Cheering on others
- Looking to lift people, not tear them down
- Effectively listening to understand
- Leaving no one behind
- Taking no more credit than you are due

Being an effective team player means that you do have to think of things as a leader would. No, you're not in charge or needing to create a vision like a leader. However, like a leader, you need to be aware of and thinking deeply about other people. One example is excelling so you don't create issues for others on the team. Another is being aware if someone on the team is struggling or behind and could use your help. Don't be like a manager who just expects them to get it done, be like a leader who is aware of people and wants to lift them.

While most of this is talking about teamwork with peers, I did mention the collaboration with your boss. One of my best direct reports did this exceptionally well. We worked remotely, different cities, yet this didn't stop her from being a team player with me. When we were having conversations, she sometimes noticed that many things were piling up on my plate. She would then always ask, "Is there anything I can help you with?" Most of the time, my answer was, "No, but thank you for asking." However, there were a few occasions where I did pass along some things for her to complete or investigate.

Some of you may be thinking that she was sucking up to me or looking for brownie points. This is far from the truth. How do I know this? It's because I knew her character, and I knew that she reached out at times to help her peers as well. This action was something that I promoted within the team that people should be willing to help others as needed. For the most part, people did when I specifically asked them to help someone, but she did it proactively without my prompting. That allowed me to know that her asking if I needed help was completely sincere as that was her character. And we've already talked about the difference between reputation and character, so you know what I mean.

There were a few benefits to her for offering this help. For starters, it gave her something fresh and different to work on. It also gave her a broader exposure to other things in the department. Most importantly, she got experience working on some things that typically are only handled by a leader. Over time, then, she got a better understanding of the kinds of things that would await her if she moved to my level. This identified new areas of knowledge she would have to learn or some skills that would need improvement. Like the Skill Set Matrix exercise, she could place these things on her development plan. Having someone ask if they can help is always appreciated. It shows a form of leadership as they are thinking about you.

Teamwork in a cross-functional department project can be challenging at times. The personalities involved always created the challenges that I saw. Some people would negatively view your department, possibly based on issues faced years ago with someone else. Unfortunately, they just can't let it go and start fresh. Other people were bound and determined to protect their turf and pushed back on some plans and refused other requests. Some people were too rigid, sticking to the "This is the way we've always done it" type of thinking. Then others would go into the project, knowing it had senior leadership's eyes, so they would try to steal the spotlight.

As you can see, none of them are operating as team players. They are going to act in a way that is precisely opposite to teamwork. They will create an unpleasant atmosphere, generate unnecessary issues, and bring risks to the project like delays or a less than optimal outcome.

If you're on a project team with people like these, hopefully, the project lead has strong leadership skills and can address these individuals. Sometimes this is very difficult as one or more of these individuals may be higher up the organizations' hierarchy than the project lead. This power imbalance may make the leader somewhat hesitant to crack down on unacceptable behaviour. Ideally, people like these aren't even in the organization but trust me; there are thousands of them out there! If you find yourself on a project team like this, it is even more valuable to operate as a team player. Find out how you can support the project lead and excel on your piece. The project lead will appreciate it greatly and hopefully provide some very positive recognition for you with your leader and others.

In closing, just remember the oft-repeated phrase, typically on sports teams, "There's no I in TEAM."

Mentoring

A mentor's definition includes both teaching and advising roles, usually the case of an older, more experienced person helping a younger, less experienced person. Typically, this is a situation that unfolds at work, but it can also happen at school or in your personal life.

In case you didn't know, Mentor was a man in Ancient Greek times mentioned in Homer's Odyssey. He was made responsible for teaching and advising Homer's son while the father was away for 20 years. This fact makes mentor the most appropriate word for the task of educating and advising someone younger!

Obtaining a mentor early in your career is a wise decision and will stay as a need during your progression. Your mentor, though, may need to change as your career progresses. You're certainly not going to get a mentor at the start of your career that would typically help people at the VP level. Conversely, the mentor you get at the outset may no longer be able to help if you pass them in the hierarchy. You should, though, be very grateful to them if they've helped you accomplish this!

A mentor is valuable in your career as they can help you avoid the many mistakes made due to a lack of experience or knowledge. You may face a problem that you just don't know how to solve. Fortunately, the mentor may have solved it before or have solved a similar issue, which you can now use as a guiding post towards a resolution. A mentor allows you to brainstorm with someone that's already been there. If you're going somewhere you've never been before, do you want to try and figure it out yourself, or do you want a map (mentor)? Most importantly, they can be impartial to your situation and help you take emotion out of the equation. Too many bad decisions get made due to feelings!

Mentors are people who will be giving you guidance over a long time. Often, there is a back-and-forth type of conversation where you may have further questions after getting an answer or guidance and applying it. Oddly enough, of all the people I provided advice to on LinkedIn, only one engaged in a full back-and-forth conversation. As well, this was the only person who said, "thank you." The others took the advice, and then it was just radio silence. More than likely, these people were expecting or just hoping for someone to offer them a job directly. Therefore, if the advice didn't include a job offer, they would just ignore it. That's certainly not something you want to do with a mentor or in a networking situation. To be clear, this doesn't mean that I was unhappy that they didn't say thank you. I know there are many people out there who don't. I raise it because it shows a small and easy way to differentiate yourself from the competition!

When you post a question for career advice on LinkedIn, it gives you the opportunity for a back-and-forth conversation, and you need to take advantage of it. Perhaps that individual could turn into a mentor. As well, you need to thank every person that responds even if you don't want to take their advice. They've gone to the time and trouble to try and help, so the least you can do is say "Thanks." You would think that the simple task of expressing thanks wouldn't be advice I have to give. Obviously, and sadly, it is. Those people are going to need an extensive reservoir of perseverance because it's going to be an uphill struggle all the way if they don't know to say "Thanks."

Please keep your mind in a constant state of thinking "win/win," which would include paying back a mentor. Most mentors do not help others with the intent of getting something back. After all, it is vital in our lifetime to be charitable with our time and skills, to help others without expecting a return. However, even if the expectation isn't there, what's the problem with reciprocating their help? You must have an "Attitude of gratitude!" If you expect them to help you grow and become more successful without looking to return the favour somehow, what does that say about your character? They are listening to you and looking to see how they can help. You should equally listen carefully to them and find out if you can do something like enabling a helpful connection for them. That will develop your skills of effective listening, networking, and leadership. The more you utilize them, the better they get, the more successful you can become!

Being Remotely Managed

The global COVID-19 pandemic of 2020 has suddenly pushed millions of people from working in an office to working remotely from home. In the winter of 2020, I was teaching on campus at Fanshawe College in London, Ontario. I was enjoying the opportunity of being back face-to-face with people as I had been remotely managing my team for the previous decade. Unfortunately, one day, an announcement came out that we'd be teaching the remainder of the semester remotely. For me, this wasn't a challenge as it merely put me back into the same mode of operation I had been in for years. However, many people greatly struggled with this change. Many of my students had never done any online learning or work and didn't like it at all. Many professors had also not done any online teaching before. Some struggled through it, while others only recorded their presentation and posted it up for students to watch on their time. The feedback from most students was that they didn't like watching a pre-recorded class. They wanted their professors to do the course live. So, moving forward, all professors taught synchronously.

I highlighted to my students that this was, in fact, a good exercise for them as many could eventually land jobs where they would be working remotely. The more they could get used to it, the better, as remote work has many challenges. I also stated that while previously there were some done remotely, the pandemic could result in many former "in office" jobs remaining as remote. Why? If a company could get, let's say, half of their employees to now work from home, they could cut office space and all associated expenses in half! This change would greatly help the bottom line, which will be necessary for all the companies that had to shut down for some weeks or months during the pandemic. This expense reduction could be a way for them to recoup some of those losses over time.

On the other side of the coin, you may see some employees asking to work remotely in the future. While there are some negatives to working at home, there are also many positives. Here are a few incentivizing examples as I see them:

1. You aren't sitting in rush hour traffic for a few hours every day or waiting for a packed bus.
2. You save money from reduced gas and parking costs. Plus, you can also save if you regularly buy your lunch.
3. If you were to start your day when you would typically leave and work until you usually got home, you could get a lot more done in a week. If you work the same hours at home as you did in the office, you gain all that travel time as extra personal time.
4. You can more easily fit in tasks at home during "work" hours because you're physically there.
5. You have a much better opportunity to focus on your work as no one is dropping by your desk for a chat. This plus assumes, though, that you're home alone because if you have other family members in the house, you can have the same chat problem.
6. Flexibility to work from anywhere! One winter, I found a house to rent for a month in Myrtle Beach, South Carolina, USA. I asked my boss if he would approve the following plan. The first week would be vacation time as it would take two days to drive there, then I wanted to relax for a while with the family. Then I would work from the house in Myrtle Beach for the next two weeks. Then take the fourth week as vacation again to cover for the drive home. Fortunately for me, my boss was a leader and recognized that this would be quite feasible. He said, "If you didn't tell anyone you where in Myrtle Beach, they probably wouldn't even notice." He was correct. No one noticed, and it was delightful working each day on the patio, under a palm tree, just a few blocks from the beach. This set-up was significantly better than working inside at home because it was freezing and snowing there!

Hopefully, your boss is someone who truly supports work/life balance and lets you juggle tasks from both during the day. In realistic terms, let's say you start working at 8 am and finish at 6 pm. And in that time, you spent 90 minutes on some household items. Should this really matter to your boss if you're doing quality work, delivering on-time, and delighting your clients? The answer from a boss who is a leader is "No." If it is an issue, then you need to find a new boss. One other key point is that work around the house cannot interrupt the completion of any required deep work. Housework can be those little breaks you need between shallow work tasks.

As stated earlier, some people worked done remotely before the pandemic, but many more will be remote afterwards. As this may be a new reality for you, there is something essential to keep in mind. You and your boss will very rarely be in the same physical space at the same time, if at all. This case was quite true in my last two corporate roles. Some direct reports I met face-to-face just once while there were five people that I never met in person. This reality means it will take much longer to build a strong connection to your boss. As well, it will take a different approach versus being in the office with them every day. Don't fall into the "out of sight, out of mind" trap and operate in silence. It's not going to be impossible to build a healthy relationship. It will just take different approaches and more time.

If this happens to you, what else do you have to keep in mind to succeed in this environment? In many ways, it's the same as if you were working in the same office as your boss. However, there are subtle differences. For starters, you must <u>remain as dedicated and professional</u> working from home as you would be working from the office. For some people, this may be a real challenge. While I did say you get interrupted a lot less at home versus the office, there is the possibility of you getting very distracted at home by non-work tasks.

Working from home calls for <u>extreme discipline</u> whereby you do so like you would at the office. This statement might sound contradictory to my saying; you could do laundry during the day. What I'm saying is that you can do laundry, but you must make sure that your job doesn't slowly start to slide, especially when there are some difficult or tedious tasks on your plate that you'd prefer to avoid!

The next important element is, ironically, <u>staying visible</u>! How can you stay visible when you're working from home and maybe even in another country? One easy way is to ensure that you are very active in any team meetings. I had some people on the team that attended every bi-weekly team call, but if you didn't notice their name in the online conference call attendee list, you wouldn't know they were there. A leader will detect this and wonder how you can consistently be in meetings but contribute nothing or ask any questions. Being silent gets noticed just as much as being active but is looked at negatively.

A second way to stay visible is to put your hand up for extra duties or projects or communities. Volunteering will give you more contact time with not only your boss but perhaps leaders in other departments (networking!). Sometimes a small team of people works on a project, but only one person presents the results. Make sure to get your hand up to be that person. You shouldn't get more credit than the others if you all contributed equally. Rest assured, though, it's easier to remember the name of the person presenting versus anyone else on the team. This fact is vital when remote work dramatically decreases the opportunity to be visible with others. As well, such visibility is critical for your boss to get their leaders' support to promote you down the road.

At times you might be remotely managed but still have a local office meaning there's the option to work from home or in the office. I'll share another story highlighting why you should go into the office for visibility, from time to time if possible. This story involves the same direct report I mentioned in the first chapter. The one who thought he should be promoted as he'd been on the job longer than others who received promotions.

In our situation, for meritocracy purposes, a recommendation for promotion could also involve the input of your leadership peers. There were a few reasons why I wouldn't recommend him for promotion. Reason number one is that if I tried with someone like him, there would have been an unwinnable challenge due to his lack of visibility with other leaders. Three of my leadership peers regularly worked in the same office as this person. Two of them had desks within 20 feet (6m) of his. Yet, they never saw him in the office. They had no idea what he was doing or contributing, and he certainly wasn't building any relationship with them. Was it a long drive for him to get to the office? No, he only lived about 7 minutes away by car yet chose to work from home continually.

To be clear, from home, he delivered two of his overarching goals: quality work and on-time delivery. However, he kept forgetting that he's compared to visible peers who where added value to their clients and the department. Sure, he could be doing the job just as well as them, but as discussed earlier in the book, this is where differentiation comes into play. The edge will go to those who are visible and building relationships. The point here is that visibility comes in many forms. It comes from being physically seen, building relationships, and being active in meetings and extracurricular activities. However, don't get discouraged if you're working remotely and unable to get into an office. Excellent visibility is still possible with making presentations and putting your hand up. It's what you should be doing in the first place, even if you were in the office every day.

By being a reliable team player, you build better relationships with your peers, which helps when working remotely. Let them know you're there to help when they need it. Then make sure to come through when they do ask. Where possible, try to make a connection with them in areas that are not just work-related. Look for things outside work that you have in common. Two people on my team built a great relationship over two years while working remotely from each other. Then, when the woman in Mexico City was getting married, she invited her co-worker from Canada to attend the wedding. Fortunately, the ability to work remotely allowed the woman from Canada to work from Mexico for a week before the wedding. Let's add that to the benefits list!

Thinking outside the box as to whether there's something new you can bring to the table. Doing this is always a good thing as it shows you're thinking in broader terms. It also shows that you're looking to add more value versus your co-workers, who just focus on doing what's on their plate. As mentioned earlier, one of my direct reports suggested adding a BPI community to the mix. Yes, communities weren't new, but having one to share BPI practices was. This move gave her wider exposure not only within our department but with those outside our area. I also got her to present on a weekly leadership video call, which elevated her visibility there. These steps turned out to be very good for her in the long run. She got moved into a 2-year development program for high potential employees. Then came out of that to lead a brand-new department.

Again, if you are remote from your manager, work at home when desired, but there is an office in your city; make sure to get into the office from time to time. The amount would depend on whether you have co-workers there or you're the only one on the team in that city. A few other leaders in the department and I each had direct reports in Mexico City. We asked them to ensure that they all came into the office at least on Wednesday. The reason being we wanted them to keep connected and perhaps even socialize after work to build better relationships.

When we had a new hire join the team, that person needed to come into the office every day in the early going. We also got the rest of the team to share being in the office Monday to Friday. In that way, the new hire always had an experienced person sitting next to them for direct and instant support. As time passed and the new person started to prove themselves, they could start working from home a bit.

Another practical reason to get into the office in person occasionally is to build or maintain relationships with people outside your department. This move is indispensable if you decide to look for a career change into another department. It will undoubtedly help your chances to move if the decision-maker in that department knows you and sees you in person more than once in a blue moon.

Finally, make sure you don't forget to keep moving forward on your self-development! There is the danger of being at home to slip into an area of complacency regarding yourself. Don't let this happen! Here's a tip. One of the benefits of working from home is that you don't have all that travel time anymore. How about scheduling self-development time into the morning and evening travel time slots? If you spent two hours travelling each day and convert it into self-development time, you could spend around 500 hours in a year. That's around the equivalent of a full-time university semester while you're working!

To summarize on being remotely managed:

- Remain as dedicated and professional at home as if you were in the office
- Do many things to stay visible
- Make sure you are a reliable team player
- Think outside the box to add value
- If feasible, get into the office regularly for relationship purposes
- Use time saved on reduced travel for your self-development

CHAPTER 7

PERFORMANCE REVIEWS

This chapter is as much for a business owner or leader conducting performance reviews as for an employee. That will be so if they've never assessed performance as described in these opening notes.

I believe that most assessments today are conducted by only measuring the "What" of a performance. Perhaps this is because it's relatively easy as metrics are involved. In truth, an equal portion of the review needs to assess the "How." This portion is much more challenging to measure as it is subjective.

What and How

Most often, performance goals set at the start of the year include specific metrics, i.e., sales target in dollars or units or percent of on-time deliveries. These metrics are the "What" in a performance review. Typically, the boss and employee determine a rating based solely on these metrics. However, to truly measure a person's performance, you should also consider the impact of the "How." Yes, the employee achieved the metric of $2M in sales this year, but how did they make that happen? I'm going to give you an example of two employees in the same role at the same company with the same performance metric target. At each step, your task is to decide who has done the better job based on the information known to that point. Then, at the end of the exercise, see if your decision changes along the way. If it changes, then think about why.

The "What and How" exercise:

- Thomas and Hailey are sales reps on the same team, and each has an annual sales target of $2M
- At the end of the year, Thomas has achieved $2.5M in sales, 25% over target.
- Hailey's sales totalled $2.1M, which is 5% over the target

Question: Based on these "What" facts, who would you say performed better?

Now let's look at "How" each person achieved their number.

Thomas: He achieved many sales by promising tight delivery timelines or agreeing to custom work. The problem was that he didn't first confirm with Operations. He often did a poor job with documenting client needs resulting in some rework requests. When Operations pushed back, he escalated to senior management that revenue was in jeopardy if they didn't deliver as agreed with the client.

Hailey: She consistently checked with various people in the Operations area regarding custom client requests, delivery timings, documentation needs and project planning. At times she even brought Operations reps to crucial client meetings to handle questions in their area of expertise.

Question: Based on these "How" facts, who would you say performed better?

Now let's look at the impact of the "How" in both cases:

Thomas: For many of his sales, Operations had to reprioritize and reallocate resources to hit his promised, tight timelines. Poor documentation resulted in a lot of back and forth with the client. In the end, even though they got what they paid for, some clients were not happy with the overall experience. As well, Operations were always stressed and frustrated. As some staff had to work overtime, and all the back and forth created inefficiencies and rework, cost overruns left a $400K profit.

Hailey: For her sales, Operations delivered the products to specification and by the agreed deadlines. Projects ran smoothly with no issues raised, and the clients were satisfied with the experience. There was very little rework required, no additional resource needs and no unexpected additional costs. These sales delivered a bottom-line profit of $600K.

Question: Thomas generated an extra $400K in revenue, but the impact of the "How" meant that Hailey delivered an additional $200K in profit; so, in the end, who did the better job?

Question: Is your final decision the same as when you analyzed just the "What," or is it different?

You would be correct if you have assumed that I worked with one or more Hailey's and Thomas's over the years. That's why this advice is timeless. These people and situations have always been there and will continue to be there. The key is to have a greater awareness of the "How" piece and handle the situation accordingly for an improved benefit for yourself, the team, and the business.

Circling Back

This section is to remind you of the process described earlier in the book. Your annual performance review's starting point is when you agreed and documented your goals for the year. Hopefully, they were written using the SMART format. Here's a tip. Throughout the year, place copies of emails or documents in a file that quantify your performance against the goals. This action is significantly more efficient than digging through all your files and emails, looking for the information in the days before your review. It will also help avoid the costly problem of missing crucial details when writing your input. Also, don't forget that when adding information to the review document, do it in SOAR story form where possible. It won't have the same amount of detail as if you were verbalizing the story, but you do that during the discussion. Following these three steps should improve your chances of getting the kind of rating you deserve.

Difficult Feedback

An unpleasant topic now, but sometimes you may receive difficult feedback. This evaluation could be constructive criticism, which, while difficult to hear, is for your benefit. In this situation, you need to avoid going into a defensive mode, as mentioned in an earlier chapter. We all have weak spots that need improving, and most reviews, if not all, will include something in the form of your development needs. It would be best to assume that this difficult feedback is accurate and fair, and you can dig into it deeper after your review. Hopefully, you already know this is a weak spot of yours, so no surprises here.

In my career, two people who reported to me could not accept difficult feedback. The first person worked for me in Canada. The situation here was his attitude, which rubbed many people the wrong way. I'd had a few conversations with him in the previous months. Then, within two days, I got calls from two internal clients. They didn't want him to speak to their external clients ever again, plus they wanted him removed from their accounts. The feedback I got was like other complaints and aligned with things I'd previously discussed with him. I now had no alternative but to put him on a performance improvement plan (PIP). I drafted the document, which now put the issue in writing and identified what he needed to change moving forward. With the PIP, there was a 3-month deadline by which he needed to adjust.

I met with him and a representative from Human Resources (HR), presented his copy of the document and discussed the situation. I closed the meeting by saying that the future was entirely in his hands. If he decided to make the changes required, everything would move ahead as usual. However, if he chose not to change, that would force me into the next step in the process. To make a long story short, as this was an attitude issue, then no surprise that he refused to accept this feedback and continued as before. Only three weeks later, I had him back in a meeting room, along with HR and an external service representative to escort him out of the building as I fired him.

The next person worked for me remotely in the US. She was in a team I inherited when moving to a new role in another department. Initially, I visited the team for a few days to get to know them, their clients, and their projects. Most of the group had been around for several years but had only recently moved into these new roles. On the other hand, she was new to the position and the company as well.

About a month and a half later, I came to realize that she, and two others, were underperforming. At this point, I started to work with them more closely on the things they needed to improve. A few months later, it became apparent that no amount of training would develop two of them in the required areas. However, she still had a chance to improve but needed to address this need more seriously. I flew to the US to meet up with these three individuals. I informed the other two that, unfortunately, I had to exit them from the business. They understood, and in some ways, were relieved. The reason being they knew they were struggling with their jobs. They had been in different roles the previous year, and when the company made structural changes, management told them to either accept these different roles or leave the business. They took the positions as they wanted to keep a "job," but weren't all that happy as they struggled in their work.

I put the third person on a PIP to get her more serious about engaging in the required development. I had an HR representative with me for the meeting and alerted him that she would probably not take this news well. I based this assumption on how she reacted to difficult but valid feedback previously. Relatively early in the discussion, she proved me correct by starting to cry then asking to leave the meeting. Upon her return, I pointed out that I believed she could still develop, which is why she was on a PIP rather than being exited like the other two people.

As with the employee in Canada, everything was in her hands as to how she moved forward. We could tell that the message wasn't getting through to her as her responses kept looping back to "No, I'm doing a good job." She was in a defensive mode and wasn't going to listen. The HR rep took over the conservation at one point to see if she would better receive the same message from him but to no avail. Let's make a long story short again. Fortunately, two months later, she decided to quit and gave me less than 24 hours' notice. She was still outraged and not accepting the feedback in any way. Like the Canada case, her chief negative influencer was also attitude.

To close on performance reviews, I want to highlight something to everyone who has direct reports. If you have someone struggling with things or making mistakes, you need to discuss it with them as quickly as possible. For starters, this ensures that they can immediately begin development to eliminate these struggles or mistakes. Secondly, if one of your team is like the two people I just discussed, you're going to need to prove multiple instances of trying to address issues if you fire them. Finally, you want to make sure they aren't making mistakes because of misunderstanding or inadequate training. The worst time for an employee to hear of issues, for the first time, is at their annual review. If your staff is hearing challenging feedback, it should only be difficult for them because you've addressed it previously, and they haven't adjusted. Yes, it's no fun giving difficult feedback, but the sooner you do it, the better it is for the employee and the business.

CHAPTER 8

LEADERSHIP

Definition

As mentioned at the start, in teaching a leadership course, I would highlight valuable lessons for my students to understand how leaders should operate. By understanding how leadership looks at people, what they need to accomplish, or the challenges they face, the students could work in a way to gain visibility and favour with their leadership. Not in a "kiss up" way, but in a properly functional and supportive way. After all, how would you expect to advance anywhere, under a great leader, if you're not doing all the right things to drive success? Why should they give you any greater responsibility or authority? In giving you a promotion, your future performance will reflect on the leader. It would be best if you gave them the confidence that you will make them proud of their decision.

As with other topics, you may want to buy a book dedicated to leadership for a deeper understanding. That should be about 10-15% of the people reading this book. For the rest of you, even if you will not become a leader in the next 5-10 years or have no desire for leadership, it's still imperative to have a view today on how they think and operate.

Here's an article I posted on LinkedIn in late 2019. It's still there on my profile, but I'm resharing it here, so you don't need to find it. There are some elements in the article that I'll expand on later.

Lead Rather than Manage People; It Benefits Everyone

I've reported to several people over the years; many acted solely as managers, and a few operated as leaders. I had direct reports for many years, and on reflection, I honestly only started leading through the latter part. That time is when the light came on for me, and I'm hoping to turn the light on for you sooner by sharing just a few thoughts on the subject.

As the headline says, if you lead people rather than manage them, it benefits everyone. Your team is happier about coming to work, while their added productivity and freedom to express themselves helps hit your goals, which benefits the company and its' shareholders.

People typically think that leaders are only those at the top who create visions and missions and below them are people managers. Organizations should promote that everyone who has direct reports needs to operate in a leadership style, and they should remove the term 'manager' from their vocabulary.

Even dictionaries have a definition of management and leadership that needs to be adjusted.

Change the Definitions

The dictionary definitions today create the manager mindset that needs to change. I checked a few online and found these definitions:

Management: "The process of dealing with or controlling things or people." "The control and organization of something, esp. a business and its employees."

Leadership: "The action of leading a group of people or an organization." "The quality or ability that makes a person a leader, or the position of being a leader."

I even found a dictionary that doesn't contain the single word leadership!

It's sad but revealing that the two definitions of management talk about <u>controlling</u> people. If you feel you must control people, you're in the wrong position.

The dictionary definitions should be:

Management: Ensuring mechanics are established and communicated, so people know what they need to accomplish and how.

Leadership: Leadership is engaging and empowering people to accomplish goals.

Manager by Default

There are many instances of people having direct reports by what I call *manager by default*. Examples (no names, promise!) of individuals I have seen are:

- People who run their own small business
- People taking the option to manage a new team or leave the business (downsizing issue)
- People who had great success in a non-management role, i.e., #1 salesperson, resulting in a promotion to management
- People who were the best of the worst options as the company needed them to fill a hole

The second element is when these folks don't have leadership, let alone management, skills. The problem is exacerbated for some people because no one will tell them they need training on how to lead (the King has no clothes!).

They don't realize how their lack of leadership abilities negatively impacts their ability to optimize their team and business success.

Manage Things, Lead People

If you control people, you stifle creativity, innovation, effectiveness and motivation. This domination means your team and the business are not optimizing potential.

You don't need to and shouldn't have to control people. You manage the standards, process, metrics, and parameters. Then you lead your people by having regular touchpoints, promoting work/life balance (not just saying it!), showing respect and appreciation. You also need to be in tune with people's career desires and help them to get there. Even if it means they would leave your team.

Leading people in this way means they will pay you back by working within those controls you manage. You respect them; they will respect the controls.

The other ingredient to this secret sauce is ensuring that people feel free to provide ideas for bigger and better ways to do things. Then you manage the changes needed to the "controls" and show your appreciation. Rinse and repeat.

Work/Life Balance

You can argue that success as a leader can be measured by how close you support your team to realize their <u>personalized</u> work/life balance. It is the essence of authentic leadership because it requires you to think of your direct reports and any family personally and not just think about the work they produce.

You hear a lot of companies and managers saying that they support work/life balance. But how many of them actually allow that to happen? How many managers even know what it truly means? And how many aren't even managing work/life balance for themselves? If they aren't managing their own, there's a good chance they aren't letting their team experience it either.

I want to come up with a better term as it looks like work is something separate from life when work is, in fact, a massive part of our life. We make connections, make lifelong friends, and for some people, work defines them. Maybe the '/' which indicates dividing work from life should be replaced with '&' to signify the connection. So, work & life balance instead of work/life balance.

Enabling work & life balance can seem complicated as the needs differ across your team. Some people may be older and empty nesters; some have young school-aged children, while some are young and single. Even if people achieve a balance at one point in time, it may not remain the same throughout the year or over time. For example, the single person gets married, or the person with young children is now dealing with their school summer holidays.

To keep it simple and consistent, I allowed my team to personalize their balance by setting three simple goals (which lay over those in their performance plans):

1. Deliver great quality in everything you do
2. Deliver on-time
3. Add value to the client whenever and wherever you can

Keep in mind; this didn't just apply to their external clients, but their internal clients as well.

When they started or stopped their day didn't matter. If they attended a school event during a weekday afternoon and caught up on Saturday, it didn't matter. Just keep hitting those overarching goals and your performance goals.

Many managers think they need to control when people start and stop their day. There is a definitive start time for many jobs, i.e., pilots (or maybe not given all the late departures I've had over the years!) I led a team spread across five time zones. How do I know if my team member in Romania has started her day on time when it's 3 am and I'm sleeping? Should I have worried about this? No. Did I need to worry? No.

On September 19, 2017, a massive earthquake struck Mexico City. Two of my team lived there, and I reached out as soon as possible. Thankfully, they and their families were all safe, as were their buildings. In talking to the first person, I could sense that something wasn't sitting right with her. Through a few questions, I found out that she felt helpless working through the day while people helped others whose buildings had collapsed on her street. I asked if she wanted to stop working and help them now, which she did. I told her to do whatever she needed to for balance. I also said if she needed some help to meet any deadlines, the team and I would help her. I then informed my second team member that she could do the same thing.

My team members were grateful for the opportunity, never asked for help and completed all their work commitments. I knew I could trust them; they had a balance that worked for them.

Self Evaluation Time

If the approach I'm sharing is in line with how you lead people today – congratulations to you and keep it up! If your way is not aligned, but you will give strong consideration to making adjustments – congratulations for being willing to learn and adapt (learning is a lifelong journey).

If you don't currently have direct reports but will be conscious of this advice, should you ever be in that position – congratulations on being better prepared than I was.

Bottom line; leading people and managing things; benefits your staff, which will help you better achieve your goals and support the company goals, making the shareholders happy. Lead Rather than Manage People; It Benefits Everyone!

There are books to provide you with multiple strategies for the early stages of leadership. It would be a good idea to pick one up for more detailed instruction once you know you'll be leading a team. One strategy I used when taking over a new one was an exercise you can, and should, perform from time to time, even if you're an individual contributor. As early as possible, when taking over a new team, I'd send out a notice regarding the discussion points in our next one-to-one meeting. I asked each person to prepare a Start/Stop/Continue list. I wanted to know their perspective on:

- Start: Is there something that you or the team aren't doing today that would help if we started doing it tomorrow?
- Stop: Are there things you have been doing to date which we should stop doing now?

- Continue: What are the valuable and important things that you're doing that we must ensure to continue?

There's an excellent chance that you will get input on all three points from everyone on your team. Why? You may find some were not started or stopped because of a reluctance by the previous manager (not a leader!) to make decisions in that area. You may find that some ideas died previously because the timing wasn't right. However, now is the time! As well, the idea might have initially required extensive manual intervention, so it didn't make sense then. However, nowadays, there is a tool, or perhaps someone on the team with specific expertise, that can eliminate 90% of the manual effort. These changes mean the idea is now entirely feasible.

Perhaps the group never provided these suggestions to the previous manager out of fear. Sadly, there are managers out there whom employees fear. For that reason, they will not make any suggestions due to what the manager may say or do. These kinds of managers should never have people reporting to them. They diminish performance <u>and</u> potential. By openly and effectively listening to the team's input, you will improve performance, enhance job satisfaction, and tap more of their potential. It will become a constant positive cycle. One crucial point, however. If you go through this exercise, you <u>must</u> be willing to find a few suggestions to address immediately. Listening to all this input and not taking any action will damage your relationship with the team. It will cause more damage than a manager who never even asks the question. They won't make any recommendations again, which then inhibits potential and makes performance suffer. It's the same as doing an employee satisfaction survey then not acting on the feedback. Everyone feels the exercise was just a farce; you wasted their time and have proven that you don't genuinely care about them.

It is now time where you should stop for an exercise. List out what would be the start and stop answers for your current role. As with a SMART goal or a DMAIC process, what data do you have to quantify these suggestions? I'm sure you know what I'm going to ask next. After you come up with the list and the data to quantify these actions, will you ask your boss for a meeting to review them? Are they someone who will be eager to listen and then act? Are they someone who will listen but probably not act? Or are they someone who won't hear you or to whom you would be afraid to make suggestions? If they aren't the first boss, eager to listen and act, my recommendation would be to find a new job!

You will hear the term "work/life balance" used at different companies, and I touched upon it in my LinkedIn article. They all pitch it the same way, but there are vast differences in how they deliver against that term. They sell it from the organization's highest level but don't honestly control how well every boss in the organization actualizes the promise. I'll share with you probably the shortest but most impactful speech given to graduating university students to illustrate the importance of them ensuring work & life balance. The address was by Bryan Dyson, former CEO of Coca-Cola, and it only took him 30 seconds to say:

"Imagine life as a game in which you are juggling some five balls in the air. They are Work, Family, Health, Friends and Spirit and you're keeping all of these in the air. You will soon understand that Work is a rubber ball. If you drop it, it will bounce back. But the other four balls – Family, Health, Friends and Spirit – are made of glass. If you drop one of these, they will be irrevocably scuffed, marked, nicked, damaged, or even shattered. They will never be the same. You must understand that and strive for it."

To declare that I supported work & life balance, each of my direct reports needed to confirm that I enabled something that worked for them individually. As so many people on my teams had different 'life' situations, I certainly couldn't create custom rules for balance for each person. This would also be challenging over time as peoples' conditions changed. To help you see this better, what do you think are the different balance needs for someone young and single versus a married person with a baby versus a single parent vs a married person with five children…? Some of them need to be at home with a sick child at times; some need to take their children to appointments during the daytime, whereas some have no other commitments, so they are willing to put in extra hours and travel extensively.

How can guidelines ensure a work & life balance when the needs are so complex across the team and change over time? I decided to give them three simple asks, in an overarching sense, for what they needed to do. If you're a leader now, you can consider using the same asks. If you're an individual contributor, you can implement these asks for yourself as a guiding light. Everyone on my team had different clients, different types of solutions, and various tasks to manage. They also had differences in their annual performance goals. However, what they all had in common were those three asks from a few pages back. I know that this is a repeated commentary, but it's important because it's about "life!"

I didn't care if they started work at 6 am or 10 am. It didn't matter if they stopped at 3 pm or 8 pm. If they needed Friday afternoon off for a personal appointment but made the time up on the weekend, it didn't matter. If they wanted to put in 40 hours between Monday and Thursday so they could head out of town for a long weekend at times, that was okay. People could operate in any way necessary for their individualized work & life balance if they achieved the three asks. At the end of the day, there isn't value in being at your desk from 9-5, Monday to Friday. The value is in best quality, on-time delivery and added client value. Do you agree?

Here's more food for thought. I believe that allowing people to manage themselves in this way makes them more productive, creative, and motivated. Their minds are freed up at work to an optimum level because they're not thinking about the struggle of juggling one rubber and four glass balls! To be clear, though, if people were not delivering against the three needs, they would be dealt with formally. The asks weren't an ongoing free pass to do whatever at work and home. This freedom is also an easy way to weed out poor performers relatively quickly!

To close this section, I'd like to share one of my favourite leadership stories. It's a concise story about a leader in the US. And even though relatively short, in the end, I wished I had worked for this individual. Let's see if you agree. And if you do, then how will that change your thinking and actions moving forward?

In 2008-09 there was a global financial crisis that was the worst since the Great Depression. That crisis started with a stock market crash in 1929 and continued for a few years. During the current financial situation, expansion was halted, some economies began to contract, and the impact on countries toppled some governments. Leadership was under pressure everywhere. This specific story is from the US, where 9 million Americans suddenly lost their jobs and unemployment hit double digits.

Overnight this manufacturing firm lost 30% of their orders. Obviously, with such a sudden and significant impact on revenues, action needed to be taken swiftly. The Board of Directors met, and I'm sure you can guess what they discussed. Yes, the only discussion was to agree on how many people they would exit from the business. Their "simple, quick and easy logic" was based fewer people being required to manufacture and ship the products as orders were down. (As an aside: I propose that "Sqael," pronounced "skeel," should be a new word to describe when people come to less than an optimal decision by using simple, quick, and easy logic.)

When the board concluded on a number to exit, they shared it with the business owner. Unlike the board, the owner didn't use "sqael" and instead thought of the impact on his employees. He told the board what the company was going to do and then shared it in a meeting with all the employees the next day. Close the book at this point and think about alternative solutions. Think in terms of impact on people.

The owner announced that he wanted everyone to take six <u>unpaid weeks of vacation</u> that year. This move would reduce business costs so that <u>every employee would keep their job</u>. The reasoning was that he wanted everyone to suffer a little rather than having some employees suffer a lot.

What happened next surprised the leadership group. Not only were all employees on board with the idea, but some even modelled the owner in their actions. As you can imagine, employees in the same company are in very different financial situations. Some were single and financially comfortable at the moment; others were late in their career, empty nesters with no mortgage, while others were married with kids and a big mortgage. Those that could afford it offered to take a few weeks of unpaid vacation from their fellow employees who would struggle financially. In a grand gesture of real teamwork, everyone suffered to the level they could manage.

Okay, if you came up with the same solution, you're brilliant! If you didn't, that's okay because I had never heard of such a marvellous solution before. In many ways, this genius idea gained a lot for the owner and didn't cost him anything, although I'm sure he also sacrificed in some way. So, although clients cancelled orders and revenue declined, costs equally dropped with all the unpaid vacation. Bottom line, the business stayed steady and healthy. I'm sure that the owner thinking of how he could protect <u>everyone</u> lead to greater loyalty, higher motivation, and improved teamwork. I don't have the details, but it would be interesting to see how the business faired after the crisis.

I wonder if he employed this procedure once more with the Covid-19 pandemic now wreaking havoc on business? I wonder, too, how many other companies during the pandemic could have used this solution rather than exiting people?

Do you agree with me? Is this the kind of leader you would like to work for? Even if you have no desire to lead others, you can still utilize this kind of leadership skill (being empathetic to others) to improve your work environment and satisfaction. For example, perhaps someday you'll be in a company or group facing a similar financial challenge, and you could offer this procedure up as a solution. You just never know.

Operating Like a Leader

Even if you do not desire to lead other people at some point in your career, it's still of great value to you to operate like a leader. What does that mean? There are many elements to being a great leader but defining them is very complicated. This challenge is why there are so many different definitions of leadership and so many books on the topic. In checking dictionaries, we find descriptions like:

- The action of leading a group of people or an organization
- The state or position of being a leader
- The leaders of an organization, country, etc.

Wikipedia has a much broader definition of leadership. It highlights how leadership approaches vary between Eastern and Western cultures. Then differ again within the Western culture, such as North America versus Europe.

There are numerous leadership styles. There's even variation within the same leader, based on the current team and situation. Sadly, some people feel you must lead by fear! After a promotion early in my career, my new boss directed me to discontinue my friendship with those I now led. I didn't understand it then, didn't 'drop' my friends and still don't understand it today. In retrospect, that advice came from someone I'm not sure had any friends and, by my definition, was a manager and not a leader. Sure, things will change with your friends at work to a degree, but I don't think you have real leadership skills if you must drop a friendship.

It's day one on the job now, and you should start carrying yourself like a great leader even if no one reports to you. You will get noticed because most of your competition for that next career step is not doing this. It's also excellent training for your future as great leaders need to keep doing this even if they've been a leader for years already.

While leadership styles will vary, as will your teams and situations, here are key elements that should remain a constant:

- Frequent self-reflection
- Continual self-development
- Service to others
- Motivate those around you
- Always "think outside your box"
- Stay current with your industry and competition
- Be a swan

Let's look at each of these.

Frequent self-reflection: You should find out early when your boss will assess your performance. Some may only do an assessment annually, others semi-annually, and others may update you quarterly. Even if they only review your performance annually, you'll have to self-reflect more frequently. Time passes quickly, and you must be careful not to ignore development because you're too busy on the job. What's fortunate for you is that most of your co-workers will get so caught up in their busyness that they will fail to self-reflect and self-develop. This lack of focus gives you an incredible advantage come promotion or new opportunity time. Besides that, to live a full life means to grow continually, and self-reflection is always the first step in personal growth.

Continual self-development: The Skill Set Matrix exercise you went through before applying for the job should highlight needed development areas. Based on that, you should be able to create a development plan on day one. Your new boss may also know what training you need, but make sure you have everything covered from your self-reflection. Don't overload yourself initially; instead, write up some SMART goals to plan out development over the next 12 months. Start with the ones with the most significant gap to the desired level of knowledge or expertise.

Service to others: The most common way to do this is to be a great team player. Please, always do your best when teamwork is involved. You need to be aware of others and to see if you can offer them help in any way. From a lunchtime conversation, you might hear that someone is struggling with a particular task or problem. Perhaps you can give them some of your time to see if you can help. Your company might have events to run or charitable work, and they need help. Make sure to volunteer! Remember, this is good practice because the differentiator between a leader and a manager is that the leader considers people, not just things. Besides that, connecting with others in this way is also a great way to build your network, which we talked about in chapter 6.

Motivate those around you: This element is linked, in ways, with service to others. Where this can come into play is on long projects where people are getting worn down. Or perhaps there have been some changes implemented that people are struggling to accept. Even if everything is fine, it's always helpful and noticeable when you walk into the room all upbeat and cheering others up!

Always think outside your box: This statement is discussed in more detail in the next chapter. For here, in summary, it means looking to get a more comprehensive understanding of the business. To do this, you need to ask questions such as:

- What is the process in the other departments I connect with?
- How does what I do impact them?
- What are they trying to accomplish, and can I come up with any ideas to help them?
- What could my group do better if we got help from other departments changing or adding to what they do?

- Are we getting enough feedback from clients, internal and external, to help improve our performance?

Stay current with your industry and competition: This is a must to develop valuable ideas or display any thought leadership level. It's a matter of continual reading and research to keep you ahead in the game.

Be a swan: That's where, no matter how difficult the situation, you look calm like the part of the swan above the water, while internally, your mind is running just as hurriedly as the swans' webbed feet are paddling beneath the surface.

To accomplish the above and be better positioned to observe your leader, it's imperative to be part of their "in-group." An in-group is not like being someone's favourite, although it is somewhat related. Typically, this is a small portion of the overall team. There is a high degree of mutual influence and attraction between the leader and the direct reports they place in this group. You get here by being noticed as a great team player, willing to sacrifice, or innovative (start/stop). All the things that leaders are looking for in people to whom they can give extra tasks, critical assignments and eventually promote. You need to be in this group to get anywhere.

Leaders are passionate and driven to succeed. They can generate excitement and build strong relationships. These things can all be part of your make-up as well, and it will get you noticed. While you may not be in a leadership position now or shortly, the sooner you start to practice leadership skills, the better off you will be. And the more you practice these skills, the more natural it will feel when you eventually have people reporting to you. And if you ultimately want to become a leader, then best wishes for much success in that endeavor!

Perseverance

This topic and the next, Motivation, are included as you will need heavy doses of both. Firstly, what you are learning from this book needs to be a lifelong pursuit, requiring perseverance. More importantly, if at some point, you are unemployed and applying to dozens of jobs, you're in great need to have this as a part of your character. I've included them in this chapter as leaders should be powerfully demonstrating both attributes.

Perseverance is defined as persisting in doing something despite difficulty or delay in achieving success. That will apply here if you have some problems learning or perfecting some of the techniques included. You should also expect there will be some lag in getting a new job or being promoted. Consider, too, if you are currently in school and would ultimately like to become something like a National Sales Director or Chief of Police, this will take several promotions that will stretch over the years. So, perseverance through difficulty and delay is critical to your success. There's no getting around it!

Perseverance played a significant role in my career. The positive side was that it helped me to get noticed then offered great opportunities. A negative, though, is that I was always getting jobs thrown at me that were all messed up. People didn't think it could be done or at least knew it would be a long and challenging road to the finish line, so nobody wanted it. However, I didn't mind taking on these projects or accounts for a few reasons:

1. I wouldn't be bored with the work given the challenges.
2. Previous experiences gave me the confidence that I would eventually be successful.
3. I knew that I could persevere because everything has an endpoint. No matter how difficult things were, eventually,

it would end, and I'd be off to another project or role or team.

To support you along the way, you also need to connect to the Motivation section's advice. No matter how strongly I felt about my ability to be successful, I still needed the motivation to make it through the expected low points where your perseverance skill gets severely tested.

To be clear, though, there is a difference between persevering on a rugged, uphill climb versus persevering with banging your head against the wall. For the former, you do timely 'temperature checks' to see if there are different ways or tools or resources to lessen the difficult path to success. The 'temperature check,' for the latter, may deem that you need to cut your losses then and there. Continuing to bang your head against the wall accomplishes nothing except giving you a concussion and headaches. There is a fine line between the two, but you must find, and not cross, that line. To help you remember perseverance, let me share a synopsis of a story from Napoleon Hill's classic book "Think and Grow Rich. (Hill 1937)!

"R.U. Darby travelled with his uncle, who had gold fever, to help dig his claim. They eventually found a vein of ore, then raised the money for the equipment to bring it to the surface. Things started well, they got their debts paid off and were very excited as everything from here on in would be profit! Not too long after, though, the supply of gold stopped as the vein of ore had disappeared. They kept digging but found nothing. Instead of persevering with a different approach they quit in frustration and sold their machinery to a junk man. The junk man, though, decided to call in a mining engineer who checked this same mine and found a vein of gold <u>just three feet</u> from where Darby and his uncle had quit digging. The junk man went on to make millions from the mine."

Besides perseverance, an equally important lesson is to engage specialists or experts or "someone who has been there" to help you with difficulties or delays. In this way, you don't need to persevere as hard or as long. So, in the spirit of those two lessons, please persevere in absorbing the information in this book. Commit to implementing what you've learned! And if you think of quitting, keep in mind that you could be three feet from gold!

Motivation

It's very appropriate that the last topic in this section is motivation. After all, when you look at everything discussed so far, the amount of work involved and how long the process will take, you're going to need motivation!

In remotely managing a team, it was a real challenge to get to know all individuals well. While I had one-to-one calls with them, saw emails and attended their project calls, it's not equal to being in the same room. So, I took the opportunity of our regular team conference calls to fill the gaps for myself. I asked for a presentation, from each of them, on what motivated them at work. This not only gave me insights into this area but helped create a connection across their remote teammates. It also gave me a chance to see their presentation skills in action. As you would expect, there were different types of motivation across the team as they were in various life stages.

The first presentation came from the only single man on the team who was relatively young. To no one's real surprise, he announced that money was his motivation at this time. During the European football season, he liked to travel to the out-of-town games with his mates to support their team. During the winter season, he wanted to go skiing in the Alps. Nothing wrong with this, and yes, I was jealous.

There was a common link across those who were married and had children. Universally, they placed their motivation on providing for their family, to give their children the best chance for a great future. I was in this group as well and still am today. Even though my children are now adults, I still want to help them out and give them the best chance for happiness and success. Please note that I listed happiness before success.

One of my direct reports in Mexico City told a very different story. She shared that one day, recently, she and a co-worker decided to go out for lunch. They both were unhappy with things in their personal lives and wanted to complain about their sorry state. On the way to the restaurant, they came across a young boy sitting on the sidewalk with several candies laid out in front of him. He asked if they would like to buy some. They wondered why he wasn't in school and where he lived. It turned out that he was trying to make a little money selling candy, which he could then share with his family, who lived in another part of town. The boy then pointed to across the street to a small box and a few other items. That is where he temporarily lived. They asked if he was hungry, and of course, he was. They immediately invited him to join them for lunch to learn a little more about his situation. Needless to say, they didn't talk about their problems over lunch. They were now motivated to move ahead with whatever challenges they faced. Nothing they were unhappy with was as awful as the young boy's situation.

In the end, we all had a reason, albeit different, for finding motivation. While the reasons were motivating, unfortunately, they do not come into play during our on-going needs for inspiration. That's why I highly recommend a book on this topic, "The Motivation Myth" by Jeff Haden (Haden 2018). As with all the books I'm suggesting, it's best to read it in full to get the context behind some of the points I'm sharing here.

While this applies to us, it also applies in a multiplier way for leaders and business owners. If you lead others, please ensure you instill in your team or company culture whatever you learn from this section. Most of the people under you won't have the awareness or ability to drive their motivation. They will be missing out on the simple tips that can help them continue moving forward at their most productive clip.

All of us will determine a goal, then design the process and routine to achieve that goal. Once you do this, Jeff recommends embracing the routine, not the goal. This approach will stop you from making choices that don't support your goals. Your focus is on the process you need to follow each day. Then, when you are working on the process, it's a matter of enjoying the feeling of success each day. Your motivation will come from this constant improvement. Motivation drives future success, and celebrating all success creates even more motivation. It's a positive cycle!

His book includes tips on having your most productive day, most productive week, and most productive mindset ever. There is also advice on how to develop and improve your willpower. This ability is essential to support perseverance and help us avoid all the other distractions that move us away from our routine. This advice nicely aligns with the 'Deep Work' book mentioned earlier. For example, in both books, to support a greater chance of success, they say to remove distraction temptations by doing things like turning off your email and notifications.

While there is substantial advice in the 'Motivation Myth' book, here's the one I liked the most. "Your goals should always help you make decisions. When you know what you truly want, then most of your decisions should be automatic. In this way, you don't need to exercise willpower or look for motivation." This process is vital because, as Dr. Travis Bradberry (co-author of "Emotional Intelligence 2.0, Bradberry and Greaves 2009) writes, "…as the day goes on, we have increased difficulty exerting self-control and focusing on our work." Therefore, the benefit of making decisions based on your goals is that it helps overcome the problems created in the last hours that occur every day.

Another point Jeff makes supports actions like brainstorming and getting a mentor. Keep this in mind, particularly if you're the kind of person uncomfortable with asking others to help or see that as a sign of weakness or failure. If this is you, he advises not to be afraid to ask for help because this act is a compliment to the person you're asking.

The obvious question you might have right now is, "How are you using what you've learned?" You will have noticed traces of what I've learned throughout this book. I've described these things in sections like Right-to-Left Thinking, Project Planning and SMART Goals. I established my end goal of selling 53,000 copies of this book by the end of December 2023. Using the thinking and planning steps, I mapped out a process for achieving that goal. Within the project plan, I have some steps that are milestones. I will do a little celebration as I complete each of these to help with motivation! I've also set myself up to be happy about daily progress. I created a simple Excel file to track my progress during the first draft (which I'm in right now). For the progress calculation, I used my 57,000-word target, 1st draft deadline of August 18 and the number of weekdays from my start date to the deadline. There were a few steps to take each day to calculate daily targets and progress. I also added Excel conditional formatting. As I updated my word count during the day, formulas updated all calculations. Once my word count exceeded the daily target, the Excel formatting changed the text and cell to red. In terms of the final word target, I also included a formula to calculate the percent of target completed (86.21% now!).

Like you, I'm not a robot, and life happens! This means that my daily target didn't stay consistent as a new average gets calculated every time I go above or below each day's mark. Some days I don't hit the target because life happens, and family is a priority. Other days I exceeded the target because I got into the groove. When things are flowing, you just keep going! Exceeding the target also increases daily satisfaction and provides the benefit of lowering the daily average moving forward. These things all help keep my motivation high on what is a long and challenging road. Writing can be a very lonely job.

It's now a week later, and I'm jumping back to this section for an update. To show you how simple it is to create an Excel sheet to track things like progress and distance to the target to help with motivation, here's a screen capture of my sheet as of today:

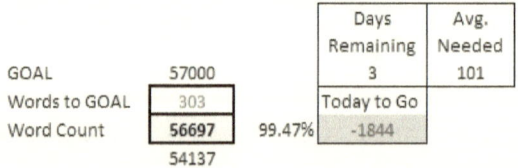

This morning I had four days remaining with a daily target of 716 as I was ahead of plan. Today was extremely productive, as evidenced by the 'Today to Go,' which is -1,844. That number means I wrote 2,560 words today. No wonder I'm tired! Now I'm left with only 303 words to my original target. With only three days left, that means I only need to average 101 per day to hit my goal! However, I plan to write at least 303 tomorrow so that I'm two days ahead of schedule. It's always a great thing if you can complete work ahead of schedule. It either allows you to deliver early and delight the client. Or it gives you extra quality check time, which will also please the client. And all of this is done without the pressure of completing work on the deadline, as many people do.

Time to stop for another exercise. Write down one goal you have currently that you are struggling to meet due to a lack of motivation. If it's feasible, use right-to-left thinking and project planning to map out the process, the plan, and the milestones. Then, start working on your process, track your progress against the target and have mini celebrations when you achieve your milestones. Finally, have your biggest celebration when you reach your ultimate goal! You'll then know how to embrace a routine and use achieving milestones as motivation to keep moving. Do that, and you'll have the proof and confidence that you can keep repeating this process and continuing to succeed in the future.

CHAPTER 9

TOOL SYNOPSIS

I hope you followed the advice early on to highlight those points that most spoke to you. The next step is typing the highlighted items into a separate document. Then creating about a 3-page synopsis from that one. If you're in the middle of doing this, then, "Congratulations!" Very late in the process, I decided it would be a good idea to provide a synopsis of all the tools I've shared. This chapter can then act as a checklist as you add these tools to your kit.

Highlighting can come into play here as well. You can use a highlighter to colour those tools that are already in your kit and need no improvement. Then you can scan the non-highlighted tools and determine which one you need to add next. When it's successfully in your kit, come back and highlight it. Use the moment as a mini celebration to aid in motivation to add another. Then it's time for a massive celebration if you're able to have them all highlighted! So, as you work through this chapter, highlight those tools in your kit. At the end of it, go back through and pick a non-highlighted tool as your number one priority to add.

So here we go with my tool synopsis for you:

It would help if you operated with a **mindset that is a combination of Kaizen + Self-reflection + Stay Curious.**

Use the **9-Box Matrix** as part of your self-reflection to determine where you stand in your current job. Then, if you're not in the top right box (Consistent Star), what do you need to do to get there?

For interviews, job performance reviews and self-reflection, always think in terms of **differentiation.**

Use the **Skill Set Matrix** process to help in self-reflection. For your next career step, how do you measure up to the skills and level of mastery required?

For your development plan arising from the Skill Set Matrix assessment, utilize **SMART goals** to steer its' completion. Use SMART for all goals that will have an impact on your success. As a reminder, you can use this tool in your personal life as well.

For both a job performance review and a job interview, make sure you have appropriate **SOAR stories** prepared. It makes it much easier for your boss or an interviewer to get a more accurate read of you and your performance when relayed in that format.

In trying to create something or set out a plan, it's beneficial to use **right-to-left thinking**. The right side for creating something for your client starts with understanding the benefits or values they want and need. In terms of planning, the right begins with the final, pre-determined deadline. For big projects, don't forget that there can be multiple deadlines for different people involved in the process.

If you already have a **Six Sigma** belt or are thinking of getting one, that's fantastic! If you're not thinking of getting a belt, you should still have enough advice in this book to utilize the process. As a reminder, Lean and Six Sigma have created a structure to follow. If followed correctly, it will lead to fixing problems and delivering improvements.

You can define **thought leadership** as "pioneering new ideas rather than following conventional wisdom." The Oxford dictionary defines it as "intellectual influence and innovative or pioneering thinking." You must focus your ideas on answering the most critical questions your target audience has today to gain real and instant traction. Doing this will differentiate you from the crowd! Just remember the Tom Hanks story and "come to work with a head full of ideas."

Diversity is quite valuable at work. Keep the example of ice cream flavours in mind and embrace diversity recognizing the added value it brings. That's part of another key message, which is "stay curious." I truly hope that eventually, you will get to the next level in this area and proactively seek people and things that are different and diverse to yourself and your way of working. The world will become a better place.

Just as much as we need to eliminate conscious bias from our mindset, we also need to eliminate **unconscious bias**. Yes, it isn't easy to control something done unconsciously. In these situations, we need our other senses to kick in and to listen to them. Please remember where my senses kicked in when there was no logical reason for me to dislike that gentleman instantly. Think through whether there may be a hidden reason for why you are taking an instant dislike, or you wouldn't hire them although they're qualified. Just like bias, which in its' worse form is racism, we need to guard against and overcome unconscious bias!

At work or in your personal life, embrace **cultural differences**, which bring diversity and spice to the environment. At the same time, remember that even with those differences in play, many **human similarities** crosscut the group. Even though the other people in the room dress differently, know other languages, or eat different foods, they, like you, want to be respected, appreciated, and treated fairly. They have the same desires, worries and fears as you. Culture is often on the outside, but you can work with or lead them based on the inside's common humanity.

Not a PM? I recommend that you try doing some **project management "light"** activities. Use right-to-left thinking to create your plan, which you then visualize in a GANTT Chart. Make a list of all the resources you'll need for the project regarding people, tools, and funds. Ensure you will have everything when required, and there is a balance between scope, time, and resource. Review your progress weekly, but also decide your RAG status and react accordingly. Don't forget to celebrate your small wins! When you complete the project, have a massive celebration because you've earned it!

In terms of **time management**, portion out a 3-4-hour chunk each day for 'deep work,' for things like innovation and problem-solving. These are the things that can make a difference for you and others. You can allocate the remaining time to 'shallow work' such as checking a social media app or checking emails we didn't need to receive. While in deep work time, **never** let yourself get distracted by social media's shallow work of instant messaging or 'pop-up' emails! The ability to consistently go deep and create more value <u>gives you a significant advantage over your competition</u> who prefer working in a shallow way.

The myth is that multitasking makes you more productive. The **dangers of multitasking** are that the opposite is true. Attempting to work on critical and essential tasks while simultaneously having open and available multiple applications and distractions will slow down productivity and impede your ability to deliver optimal results. People who multitask all the time can't filter out irrelevancy. They can't manage a working memory. They're chronically distracted!

You can think of **persuasion and negotiation** as siblings. They are from the same family, but there are differences. Persuasion involves the action or process to get someone to do something or believe in something. In comparison, negotiation is more like a give-and-take situation where two parties try to arrive at a contractual agreement. You can't go through a career or life without the constant need for concrete persuasion and negotiation skills. So, the more you can learn about these things, work on them, and perfect them, the better off you and those you interact with will be.

Optimal verbal communication requires a robust two-way process. The perfect verbal message is diluted if, on the receiving end, the other person is not listening effectively. On the other side of the coin, **effective listening** can determine if the verbal message is less than perfect. Not all the time, mind you, but if you are listening effectively, you can pick up if specific details are missing or the message is becoming mixed. This reason is why, of the two parts of the process, listening skills are far more critical. The best listeners are active, not passive, in that they are focused on <u>understanding</u> what is said. To optimize focus means that while listening, you are not trying to formulate a response.

Networking is the process of interacting with other people to exchange information and develop professional or social contacts. The most important word in that sentence is "exchange." You must always consider networking to be a two-way street. If you think it's a one-way street, then you'll find a dead-end at some point soon.

Being a **team player** to create the best **teamwork** environment means things like sacrificing for others, giving credit where credit is due, and having an awareness of others. As a team player, you never look for opportunities to put yourself above others. Your thoughts and efforts are focused on total team success and not your success.

A **mentor's** definition includes both teaching and advising roles and is most usually the case of an older, more experienced person helping a younger, less experienced person. Seeking out a mentor is wise early in your career and will stay as a need during your progression. You should keep your mind in a constant state of thinking "win/win," which would include paying back a mentor. Most mentors do not help others with the intent of getting something back; however, what's the problem with reciprocating for their help?

You must remain as dedicated and professional working from home and **remotely managed** as you would be working from the office. You need to avoid your home's distractions, which calls for extreme discipline whereby you work at home like you would at the office. Ironically, the next important element is to get into a local office if possible and 'staying visible'! Make sure you're seen as a solid team player and think outside the box to add value. Finally, consider using the time saved on travelling to spend on self-development.

In a **performance review**, the impact of **how** can often matter more than the metrics of **what** you accomplished. Hopefully, your performance objectives were written in the SMART format, and you can relate your success in achieving these goals through your SOAR stories. When receiving **difficult feedback**, please don't go into a defensive mode, but effectively listen as it may be this feedback that later propels you in your career.

If you ever have people reporting to you, please be their **leader** and not their manager and definitely not their manager by default. **Leadership** is not only being attentive to things but also, and more importantly, to your people. Be like the leader who asked everyone to suffer a little instead of picking a few to suffer much.

Even if you do not have anyone reporting to you, **operate like a leader**. Leaders are passionate and driven to succeed. They can generate excitement and build strong relationships. These things can all be part of your makeup as well, and it will get you noticed.

No matter how high the mountain, no matter how thick the wall in front of you, no matter how far the road ahead, **persevere, persevere, persevere**!

Embrace the routine, not the goal. When you embrace the routine, you stop making choices that don't support your goals. Don't keep the goal in mind; focus on the process you need to follow today. You need to find the right process, work it and enjoy the feeling of success and **motivation** from continuous improvement. Then, in recognition of this improvement, **motivation** for the next step is created by celebrating all success.

CHAPTER 10

HOW TO MAKE IT ALL WORK

So, there you have it, 28 points to lock into memory and work on when it's appropriate for you. Obviously, like anything new you need to learn, you're not going to accomplish everything on day one or even within month one. What you need to do, then, is map out which items are a priority for you to learn and develop, then craft a plan. Ideally, you use project management light and right-to-left thinking to create your plan. That will put you underway with 2 of the points already!

Although I didn't list it as one of the 28, an overriding point to remember is that "It's your job to drive your career!"

Let's get all those points into a single view:

- ✓ 9-Box Matrix
- ✓ ATS, HR and the Interview
- ✓ Cultural Differences Human Similarities
- ✓ Dangers of Multitasking
- ✓ Differentiation
- ✓ Difficult Feedback
- ✓ Diversity
- ✓ Effective Listening
- ✓ Kaisersc: Kaizen + Self-reflection + Stay Curious
- ✓ Leadership
- ✓ Mentor
- ✓ Motivation
- ✓ Networking
- ✓ Operate Like a Leader
- ✓ Performance Review (What and How)
- ✓ Perseverance
- ✓ Persuasion and Negotiation
- ✓ Project Management Light
- ✓ Remotely Managed
- ✓ Right-to-left thinking
- ✓ Six Sigma
- ✓ Skill Set Matrix
- ✓ SMART Goals
- ✓ SOAR Stories
- ✓ Team Player and Teamwork
- ✓ Thought Leadership
- ✓ Time Management
- ✓ Unconscious Bias

Some of these points you need to always keep in mind. Those are mindset, effective listening, time management and dangers of multitasking. You will put others into play on a scheduled basis like Performance Review, 9-Box Matrix and SMART goals. Then others will come and go into use as the occasion arises. Quite often, as well, you will need to use multiple points simultaneously. Which combination you use will depend on your circumstances at the time.

I certainly can't cover all the occasions and combinations, but let's look at a few as an example. In this first instance, you apply for a new job (it doesn't matter if you currently have one or not). The process you follow would look something like this:

1. Set up a **Skill Set Matrix**, list all the required skills and the desired mastery level from the job posting. Undertake self-reflection to recognize where your strengths align so you can ensure to highlight those in your resume, cover letter and later an interview.
2. Start picking out your applicable **SOAR stories** that will support the items above. Make sure there is evidence of some of the stories in your resume.
3. Is there an opportunity here for you to do some **networking** to help your cause? If this role is within your current company, there's naturally a chance. If it's not, check LinkedIn to see if any of your connections work there. It can give you an edge if your contact can forward your resume and vouch for you with the hiring manager. Look for every possible advantage, no matter how small!
4. In preparing for your interview, think of what can **differentiate** you from the other candidates. You might think this is difficult because you don't know the competition. While that's true, you do at least know that they're going to have a similar skill set to you. You also need to review the

critical items of **persuasion** and make sure you work them into the conversation. Finally, please don't forget about the importance of researching the company plus preparing up to 5 questions.
5. During the interview, you must ensure that your **effective listening** skill is working. I've interviewed people who answered entirely unaligned with my question. Feeling confident that the question was straightforward, it indicated that they weren't listening carefully. Perhaps it was nerves, but these little things will make a difference in a decision.
6. Ensure that through the entire process, from the application to meeting the receptionist to the interview and follow-up thank you, you **operate like a leader**. Make sure that this quality shines through.
7. Throughout the process, use completing each step as **motivation** and a confidence builder for the next one.

This job posting may have been internal, and, unfortunately, you weren't selected. If you would apply again, there's no harm in asking the hiring manager why you didn't get picked. Ask them what you need to improve upon to be selected the next time around. You'll either know what must go into your development plan right away or that this is a manager for whom you wouldn't want to work. A closing point to all of this, if you don't get the job but are continuing to apply for other jobs, then you need to add **perseverance** to the list!

For another example, let's say you've been at your job for a long time and feel that you're performing well. However, there have been a few promotions in your area, and you're always bypassed. Well, "It's your job to drive your career." As above, when success isn't coming your way, you need to have a conversation with a few people. It would be best if you started with your boss as, in terms of promotions, they are the decision-maker. Starting here will either lead you to update your development plan or to know you've hit the ceiling here and need to move elsewhere. You could even ask if they use the **9-Box Matrix** for succession planning. If they do, then the next obvious question is, "Which box am I in?" If they don't, you can explain this model to your boss and ask the question again. You could also have a conversation with some of your peers to get their perspective. Is there anything they see from their relationship level that perhaps you need to work at improving in the future? I'll remind you again to ensure you're employing **effective listening** skills during these conversations. If you do get feedback that says a promotion could be in your future, make sure to follow the advice given. To ask for advice in this way and not follow-up on it will kill any potential you may have had for a promotion. If you don't think this ever happens, go back to the chapter on the 9-Box Matrix and reread the actual example from my leadership experience.

For a final example, let's say you have a **performance review** coming up in a few months. What would be ideal is if you wrote your performance objectives in **SMART goals** format. Great if they are, but if they aren't, then how could you form your objectives in this way? In doing this, you can now better create **SOAR stories** to competently demonstrate the **"what and how"** of your performance to highlight impact. Sure, you got things done, but **differentiation** versus others is your performances' bottom-line impact on the business. Don't forget to review your notes on **persuasion and negotiation**, and you will be well-armed for the review!

I trust that these few examples ably illustrate that individual situations can utilize multiple advice elements. Also, you can use single elements in numerous situations. That should confirm my opening statements, which I'll repeat here. One of the best things is that all the different advice types are not locked to a specific job, department, company, or industry. The advice applies everywhere! This information is what we call transferrable knowledge and skills, meaning that you can take it and apply it no matter where you go in your career. You can even use most of the information in your personal life as well. This fact creates even more value for your time and effort to read and absorb this material. It will repay you a thousand times over. Another important aspect is that this advice is timeless. No matter how many years from now someone picks up this book, things like leadership, planning, self-reflection, and skill development will still be just as valuable and relevant then.

Do you agree?

CHAPTER 11

WHERE TO GO FROM HERE

Congratulations on working through all the material! I hope you took very relevant notes and completed the exercises as you went along. As a recap, and for reference, here are all the exercises and the pages where they are found:

- ✓ Pg. 33 – Individuals answer two questions, and Business Owners or Leaders create a 9-Box Matrix and answer four questions
- ✓ Pg. 36 – What differentiates you from the other job applicants or your competitors for a promotion?
- ✓ Pg. 45 – Create a Skill Set Matrix to assess yourself against the next job
- ✓ Pg. 53 – Write at least one SMART goal for work or life

- ✓ Pg. 56 – Write at least one SOAR story
- ✓ Pg. 76 – Create a spaghetti diagram for making a coffee
- ✓ Pg. 92 – Thought Leadership review
- ✓ Pg. 99 – List out how you want to be treated at work
- ✓ Pg. 139 – Set up or update LinkedIn profile
- ✓ Pg. 156 – What and How questions
- ✓ Pg. 170 – List your Start and Stop ideas for your current job
- ✓ Pg. 174 – Guess CEO action
- ✓ Pg. 187 – Lack of Motivation
- ✓ Pg. 188 – Highlight the tools in your kit

If you haven't completed the exercises, do so in conjunction with your priority list for what you will work on. If you've completed all your exercises, look at your situation today and decide which actions are a priority for you to take. Is it to find a new job? Are you working on a project that isn't running smoothly? Are you being left behind while others are getting promoted? Then, as outlined in the previous chapter, determine which of the tools you need to bring into play. Are you confident with your ability in each and can start mapping out a plan and moving ahead? Or are there one or more tools you need to add or improve first?

You may feel that you can take this information and move forward on your own. Even so, consider if you should also find someone who could act as a coach or mentor. I believe that we are always more successful when we have others by our side.

In closing, I wish you all the very best in your future. It will be brighter if you leverage the advice shared. I want everyone to win with what they've learned, and you should all be able to win. When you do, please share your success with me via a quick email to winitdriveit@gmail.com. Please also feel free to connect with me on

LinkedIn (www.linkedin.com/in/martylateralthinkerdupuis/) so that I can follow your progress. I want to share in the knowledge of your success and toast it. That's what will help with my motivation to keep moving forward!

Another Book by this Author

"You Packed a Screwdriver?" Our Expat Adventure in Europe and Beyond

Enjoy the family journey inside Buckingham Palace and to places like Paris, Monte Carlo, and Cyprus. Many readers who also worked internationally comment on how it brings back fond memories of people they met and the places they visited.

Available on all Amazon websites.

Win It! Drive It!

SUCCESS LOG

Date:
Success:

Date:
Success:

Date:
Success:

Date:
Success:

SUCCESS LOG

Date: **Success:**
Date: **Success:**
Date: **Success:**
Date: **Success:**

Win It! Drive It!

SUCCESS LOG

Date:
Success:

Date:
Success:

Date:
Success:

Date:
Success:

ABOUT THE AUTHOR

Martin, known by most people as Marty, worked for The Nielsen Company for 33 years. He may have been the only person in Nielsen's history to have worked end-to-end in the business. He started in Data Collection then had stints along the way in Operations, tech department through to client-facing sales and service roles.

Since his Nielsen time ended, he became a part-time Professor in the Lawrence Kinlin School of Business at Fanshawe College in London, Ontario. As well, this is now his second book. The first is entitled "You Packed a Screwdriver? Our Expat Adventure in Europe and Beyond". That book covers the three years Nielsen moved him and his family to Oxford, England.

On a personal level he, and his wife Caroline, are now empty nesters as their children, Kenneth (university) and Emma (copywriting and market research career), have moved on. The house isn't too deserted as they still have the two cats they brought back from England, plus two dogs.

Martin likes to share two small but powerful words that have ended up in the mindset suggestion; "stay curious!"